Your First Dollar

Choose Your Market
Build Your List
Make Your First Dollar
Inside Thirty Days

Ed Dale

30 Days – Your First Dollar

Printed by:
90-Minute Books
302 Martinique Drive
Winter Haven, FL 33884
www.90minutebooks.com

Published in the United States of America

Book ID: 161205-00632

ISBN-13: 978-1542998987
ISBN-10: 1542998980

Here's What's Inside...

Introduction

30 Days – Your First Dollar!

The idea for this book was planted more than 12 years ago, when I had just sold my business and I found myself in New York at Starbucks in Trump Tower. It was the day after the second season of *The Apprentice* had wrapped and I was sitting at the Starbucks on the mezzanine level. I was reading a book I just picked up called *How to Write a Novel in 30 Days*, which turned out to be a book about National Writer's Month.

The title intrigued me, I'd always wanted to write a book. At the same time (SQUIRREL) I was also reading an unauthorized biography of Steve Jobs. I was also feeling pretty good; I'd also just sold one of my businesses!

I was sitting there thinking about all these things: *The Apprentice*, National Writer's Month, where you write a novel in 30 days and Steve Jobs cry to the original Mac Team "Let's make a dent in the universe. It got me thinking…, making money online was all about "Make Money by selling my stuff on how to make money to other people". I started to think, "What if I could show people how to make $1 online in 30 days?"

The Challenge was born right there and then in Starbucks at Trump Tower and now, 12 years later, over 400,000 people have gotten their start on an online business with *The Challenge*. This book is a culmination of all the lessons learned while teaching *The Challenge,* with the bonus of having all the latest groundbreaking research on behavioural psychology and neuroscience making it easier than ever for you for you to make your first dollarregardless of your learning style and current situation.

Have a look where we are today. Look at job security, well there isn't job security. The only way you can be certain you know where your next money is coming from is if you're in control of the source—if you're captain of your own ship. Starting your own business has always been considered a risky thing to do. Now, it's the only way is for you to be totally in charge. You should be the only one capable of firing yourself from your own business. Believe it or not, that's probably a goal you should have at some point in time.

People say, "What about the risk?" What you'll learn in this book, with the tools, technology, and the implementation research that's available to you - which we've distilled down to key action points in this book - starting a business on the side and growing its revenue to replace your day job income has never been more achievable, faster, or less risky than ever before.

The other reason I'm excited to share this material with you is I think if you're going to design a business for yourself, it should be fun for you. Who wrote the rule that said it couldn't be fun? One of the biggest reasons it's not fun is you're trying to follow somebody else's plan. As you'll discover later in this book, there are different types of entrepreneurs. Some of you reading this will love the idea of creating videos for your tribe. Some of you reading this would rather slam an appendage in a car door at just the thought of standing in front of a camera and you'll be miserable in the process of trying.

You're going to learn about your eOS, (your entrepreneurial operating system). If you don't get the correct eOS for you—which is a play on the word iOS (your phone operating system)— despite your best efforts, you'll fail. If you go against your core wiring, you'll make yourself miserable. The flip side is install the right eOS for you and you'll achieve more in the next 30 days than you thought possible.

The other reason for to write this book is my desire for you reading it to understand the difference a $100,000 business makes. I was traveling earlier in the year on a subway to New York up to watch the musical *Hamilton*. I noticed this guy staring at me a bit. As I went to get off he got up, came up to me and asked me, "Are you Ed Dale? Your Challenge changed my life!" It was extraordinary, I was thousands of miles away from my home and somebody recognized me on the subway.

At the ProBlogger Conference on the Gold Coast in Australia, a mother and her college-aged daughter approached me and said, "Ed, I just have to thank you. I was at rock bottom, just been divorced and lost my business and had a young daughter to get through school. I did *The Challenge*, and thanks to you, I was able to build my business back up and put my daughter through University."

I mention this not to blow my own trumpet—and I grant you, I sound a bit obnoxious—but to explain why I do this work. Look, the millions and the flashy cars, all well and good, and quite true, but I know the real difference creating a $100,000 business in the next 12 months can mean to you. It may not be sexy and I'd sell a lot more copies of this book if I highlighted my students who made a million dollars in those same 12 months.

I know if you apply the lessons in this book, a $100,000-a-year business is totally realistic and that's if you're only working part-time. I know what a real difference an extra couple of thousand dollars does to the family budget each month. That's what I want for you.

Enjoy the book! I know it will convinceyou to realize, if you've tried to start your own online business and it hasn't worked out, it's because you've used the wrong operating system.

It's not your fault.

Most of the productivity advice you've ever read is dead wrong for entrepreneurs like you. I'll explain why this is later in the book, and it's a revelation. Based on this, you're going to choose a market and get more done in a month than you dreamed possible. You are going to yourself up to work in a market you're passionate about and earn your first dollar and then more.

I hope this book inspires you to create a business that within a year replaces your income and gives you flexibility, freedom, and fulfillment, not to mention fun to live the life you deserve.

When you do, I hope you let someone else know there's a different path and you show it to them.

To Your Success!

Ed Dale

Why Don't More People Have Success Selling Online?

If you've picked up this book, you've probably tried making money before. This may not be the first time you're considering creating a business and branching out on your own. For many of you, this is not your first rodeo. You've always had the streak of an entrepreneur, but for whatever reason, you're not where you want to be. This is the story of hundreds of thousands of students of *The Challenge* over the last decade. This book is going to show you why the deck has been stacked against you and you don't know why. I'm so excited to show you.

Most people are working in a job that chooses them. A lot of people who do *The Challenge* are sick of the business they're in. Let's face it, most of us picked our career when we were a teenager. Or worse, we're just fulfilling the wishes and visions of your parents. You didn't have much of a say. You may be very successful and at that top of your field. The trouble is, the view isn't that exciting. Worse, with the responsibility you have, you're working 60 hours a week. To put it bluntly, you're miserable. There must be a better way and the good news is you're reading it now.

Most of you want to be your own boss. In a massive study we conducted a couple years ago, one of the key reasons people want to have their own business is they want to be the one who make the calls and reaps the benefits. You don't like being handed a bunch of poo from above and be forced to dance to someone else's tune. You don't have a sense of being in control of your own destiny and it's eating you slowly from the inside. Thank goodness there's a solution.

You might be in a rut with your existing business. Quite a few of you made the leap into doing your own thing, but it's plateaued. You've got the feeling of treading water. You're experiencing the feast and famine effect of servicing and getting clients. Maybe you already have an online business and it's just not growing like you hoped.

I'm glad you're here. Many people use *The Challenge* as spring training. The opportunity to review everything and concentrate on the fundamentals. You're not going to waste your time and you know how you struggle with outsourcing and getting the right people on your team. We're going to solve that straight up.

A Thriving Business in a Topic You Love!

This book's going to help you design and architect a business that delivers constant cash flow, building up to $100,000 in the first 12 months. I'll explain why this is such a key number later in the book. I want it to be in a market you love and you are thrilled to work in each day. You love telling your friends about your new business and you're making a real difference to your tribe's lives. Working when you want in the style you want.

Of course, one of the ways you could make double the income is work double the hours. This is not a good idea. I think the idea of a completely passive business is also complete rubbish. You go backpacking for 12 months and I guarantee you'll come back to a smoking ruin. You should be able to go away for a few weeks and you should only do the stuff you love doing.

I want the businesses we are building here to be fun. It'll stretch you; there'll be challenging days. This is not a Barbie movie. However, the whole point of doing your own thing is to architect a business the way you want to do it. My Aussie marketing colleague, James Schramko, manages his entire thriving business between surfing sessions on his mobile phone.

He makes sure if there is something to be done, he creates a framework to work in Slack, an awesome team communications program designed for mobile.

Dean Jackson, who you'll be hearing a lot about throughout the course of the book, has designed his business so, in theory, he could put on a big pair of mittens and he'd still be able to do his work. He's the cow that's producing the milk. He's not really a cow, I've switched into using one of his metaphors. He wanders the field eating grass and at the end of the day wanders into the shed to be milked. His team handles the pasteurizing of the milk, the transport, the bottling, the distribution, and the sale of the milk.

Too many entrepreneurs are trying to do it all. This is stopping them from delivering anything. "Now, Ed, are you going to talk to me about outsourcing? Please don't. I know." When I bring this up at any of my workshops, people get angry. I get it. Here's the thing, there's one thing you don't do that makes all the difference in building a team. No outsourcing course teaches this because the excellent people who are great at outsourcing make up about 3% of entrepreneurs. In this book, I'll reveal why and it'll change everything for you.

Solve Your Tribe's Problems, Help Them Get Where They Want to Go and Get Paid Well for It!

Here's a big point I want you to understand. You don't have to be an expert to help your tribe solve their problems and get them where they want to go. If you're constantly identifying cool people doing interesting things in your niche, your influence grows. Oprah became the highest paid TV personality through her skills with identifying interesting things for her audience they would appreciate and learn from. She brought the experts to her audience and her influence became legendary. If your book was talked about on Oprah, you had a guaranteed *New York Times* bestseller.

I'm going to show you the way the experts in your niche are going to love talking to you, how simple checklists on how to solve a specific pain in your market will get you building your tribe as fast as possible. It won't happen overnight, but it will happen.

Having Fun!

There's no point doing any of this if you're not enjoying doing it. It may be hard to believe right now, but you can wake up excited to get in and help your tribe. It's because we've designed a business you want to be in where you're in control, doing just the things you want to do. You want to be able to work from anywhere. One of the great things about an online business is you can run it from anywhere.

I once interviewed Mary Bartnikowski, the publisher of *Vagabond* Magazine. She was speaking to me on Wi-Fi from a small tea shop in Nepal. She was publishing her magazine and photographing the world. She was not making millions, but her business covered her outgoings and allowed her to travel where she wanted. Last time I checked, she was teaching photography and yoga and helping people organize their own travel adventures from Hawaii.

I'm writing this on my iPad Pro in one of my favorite coffee shop haunts. Just being able to work wherever is awesome. I sometimes like working in public libraries just for a change of scenery. This flexibility is one of the first tangible benefits you'll get in your business.

The Elephant in the Room

I think you will believe me when I say one of the most frustrating things is seeing the process working for someone else but it doesn't work for you. Here's the elephant in the room. You've tried this before. You've followed the steps. You may have even tried *The Challenge* and it just hasn't worked for you in the same way as the person who created the course or the YouTube video you're watching. This problem has obsessed me over the past few years. In the last two years, I finally cracked it, and in this book, I'll show you why it's happened to you and how you can fix it.

Life happens. Something comes up and you never come back. You start off earnestly and at some point, life gets in the way. Do you know how many times I've stuck with a New Year's resolution only to have it bust open at Easter? All those chocolate Easter eggs, yum. You get busy at work, you have a massive project due, the kids are at their end of the year concerts. This could be good stuff, like vacations and holidays. Or bad stuff, like a tragic event. In the end, all of this derails the best-laid plans.

I wish I could say these will stop after you read this book. That would be awesome but false. However, what if we accepted that stuff happens (see how I cleaned that up) and we had a system which took this into account and could get you back on track in just 60 minutes? Doesn't that make sense? Just like getting your smartphone to start working again properly by turning it off and on, we need to create an entrepreneurial operating system allowing you to reboot.

Will you waste your time committing to something only to have it fail? Thirty-five percent of you reading this have a very specific challenge. How do I know it's 35% of you? I'll reveal shortly. You love researching your market, you love learning about all this business stuff, you love reading this right now. You'll fill out questionnaires. You love the planning and research, but when it comes to pushing the button to select a market to commit to, pushing the button on a Facebook campaign, or hitting publish on your funnel, you freeze.

"What if it's not right? What if it doesn't work? I need to be certain this thing is going to work. I'm sick of doing things that don't work." You end up not starting and you go back to more fact finding. Look, this is not something to be ashamed of. I wish I had that fact checking instinct. I'm more of a YOLO person and hopefully-the-mess-will-be-cleaned-up-later type of a guy. However, you can only be right or wrong in hindsight.

There's no way of knowing if the market is right unless you get in there and test it. Same with those funnels and marketing campaigns.

What if there were a way to harness all the fact finding and research to get you moving forward with a level of certainty? Good news, you just need the right operating system installed. If you used my personal operating system it'd be a disaster. Read on.

"I Don't Want to Be a Guru!"

One of the great attractions of an online business is you don't have to deal with people. It may be a surprise to you, but I'm happiest when I'm by myself. I'm an introvert at heart. I'm comfortable, in fact, I love speaking to other people on stage or in video, but I struggle a bit one-on-one with people I don't know. It turns out when we did our study and compared the characteristics of different types of entrepreneurs, being comfortable in front of a crowd or a camera suits only about 60% of you. Forty percent of you would prefer to be behind the camera.

Here's the killer thing: the truth is you're wired this way. It's not something you can change. You may be one of the many entrepreneurs who've made themselves miserable trying to be someone they're not. Here's the good news: you don't have to be a guru. You don't have to be in front of the camera. One of my most successful students of all time creates coaching programs for parents who volunteer to be kids' sports team coaches. They operate under a pseudonym, just like Sting, Bono, and Elton John, and have never had their face anywhere. We need to design a business that suits you. If you don't want to be the face of your business, you don't have to be. We will design a business just right for you.

Everything You've Read About Productivity is Wrong... For You

Here's the problem, if you're an entrepreneur, and if you've gotten this far, have you noticed how you've struggled to implement a productivity system that sticks? One that works for you and makes you feel in control of the situation? There are only 3% of you reading who will answer yes to this question. That's right, 3% of you. This was perhaps the most dramatic finding of our research. The entrepreneurial profile is, literally, the opposite end of the spectrum to those who can maintain and keep a productivity system. All those books, Daytimers, apps, and courses and nothing sticks. It's not your fault. The truth is, the very thing that makes you an entrepreneur is the thing which will keep you from ever implementing a productivity system.

What does this mean? Is it all hopeless? Am I to feel out of control and redlining forever? Fortunately, no. You just need the right type of entrepreneurial operating system installed. You also need a system created in post-World-War-Two Japan and perfected by a bunch of software nerds who realized there had to be a better way. I've been using this with my clients for the last two years and, bluntly, this is the most important work I've ever done. The difference it creates in how you work is game changing.

Learning from *The Challenge*

How did I figure all this out? Truth is, I figured very little of this. I was extremely lucky to have the largest group of online entrepreneurs on the planet, my awesome challengers. I was exposed to a remarkable test which allows you to discover and work to your strengths and spent the last few years developing some very successful software for mobile devices. It was the crazy intersection of those disconnected worlds which helped me figure out the concept of an entrepreneurial operating system and, crucially, the fact there are four types of operating system.

Why did some people fail and some people succeed with the Challenge? While it was very gratifying to see the number of people who were starting *The Challenge*, for me it was always about implementation and finishing that was important. The more people who finished each year, the better. The trouble is, the success rate for your standard online course is less than 5%.

The MagCast course we created a few years ago had an industry smashing rate of 33% of people publishing a MagCast at the end of the course. The trouble with this is 67% didn't. Not that they were unhappy, refund rates were at an all-time low for this project, people loved the program, but for whatever reason, life got in the way.

The 4 Types of Entrepreneurs and The Way They Act is Super Different

As it turns out, there are four core types of entrepreneurs and they all act very differently. You try to follow a course created by a different type of entrepreneur with a different eOS, entrepreneurial operating system, and if you try to follow their steps to the letter, you'll find it incredibly hard, demotivating, and worse, your self-confidence will take a big hit, making it harder to saddle up for the next thing.

If you know what your eOS is, you can translate. You can still do the course, but now you'll know how to modify it so it becomes much easier for you to implement. I just wish I'd discovered this earlier in *The Challenge*. Fortunately, we know this now and this book is going to help you figure out what type of operating system you need. We'll install it correctly and get you the right apps for you to be successful and act with an ease you haven't experienced before.

Installing Your eOS—The Entrepreneur Operating System

Every productivity system you've tried has not stuck. There's a reason for this. Why haven't productivity and organization systems stuck for you? It turns out the vast majority of entrepreneurs are wired to be anti-process. They're good at finding shortcuts and 65% of us suffer from severe "squirrel" syndrome. We're like Larry, my dog, when he sees a squirrel. It doesn't matter what he was doing before, when he sees a squirrel, he's chasing the squirrel.

I'm one of the 65% who is in this category. Here's the thing you need to realize. All of us can make awesome entrepreneurs, we just must have the right operating system installed. We need to stop trying to work on our weaknesses and focus on and celebrate our strengths. Entrepreneurs are unique to 5% of the population. Once you realize this and install the correct operating system, everything changes.

The vast majority of people work very differently than we do. This is why outsourcing and managing people has been so hard for you. The people who create productivity systems are the opposite of entrepreneurs.

Note, they are entrepreneurs too, they're just the super rare—three in every 100 entrepreneurs who exhibit the characteristics of these productivity experts.

Nobody's wrong here. This is not something you need to fix. In fact, once you realize you'll never be a productivity expert and accept your operating system, you'll save so much creative energy and start to really enjoy what you're doing.

Why Working on Your Weaknesses is Crazy

When I first started working with the Kolbe Index (I'll explain what this is in a tick), the thing that slapped me upside the head was hearing Kathy Kolbe, the founder, talk about wasted energy as someone acting against their inherent nature. This was a revelation. See, I'm learning every day, too. I was working with a private client a couple years ago, and she was in a niche which would be perfect for a YouTube channel; I mean *Perfect*.

I was super excited and created an entire strategy for her. When I presented the concept in our weekly session, I could hear the hesitation. She understood my reason, and I figured— completely incorrectly, as it turns out—she'd get used to the video. After all, I found it super easy to do video, she just needed to work at it. She really tried, but doing the videos made her miserable

If only I had known what I know now. Her operating system was suited to writing, not video. When I'm working with a private client, I make sure I get them to do a Kolbe Index so we can design a business they'll enjoy. By the way, video was crucial in this market, so she started writing scripts, which she loved. We got people on Fiverr, a website that allows you to hire people to do work for you for five dollars, to do the slides and voice over to go with them.

I'm creating this book through a combination of being interviewed and when I'm typing I've created a game of typing in short sprints, which appeals to my squirrel-like nature. More on this later.

Once You Act in Alignment, Everything Hard and Energy-Sapping Becomes Easy

When your operating system's installed, everything becomes easier. You'll still need to work, and being stretched and challenged is a key part of this process as well. There's never been a better time to start an online business and work with people who are great where you are not. When you architect a business, like we're going to do now, you create it so you'll eventually only do the things you love.

Sure, right now you may have to do everything, but at least we can make a game out of the areas you're not so good at. For example, my timer just went off so I should stop typing and I get to play 10 minutes of *Clash Royale* as my reward.

Let's Look at the Alternative

I read an article in the *Herald Sun* just the other day, which is my local newspaper. It pointed out the highest paid person who is paid a salary is a neurosurgeon. Neurosurgeons earn over a half a million dollars a year.

It occurred to me that people think, "I'll be a doctor and I'll make a whole bunch of money." Think about the path to a doctor; in The United States, you need to start doing extracurricular activities, you need to be starting to study and taking tutors from the age of 10. You basically don't have a life from the age of 10 because for you to get into the right medical schools, for you to be able to earn the big money as a neurologist, you must be in the top .01%. Not 1%, .01%.

From the age of 10, you haven't had any sort of life at all. Then you have seven years of residency and working 36-hour punishment shifts. The first year out after literally 15 years of study, education, going to college, and residency, the average wage for a doctor is $72,000. That's right, $72,000 and, by the way, your college debts are in the multiple six figures.

This is the journey of a doctor. I'm asking you to give me a year of working 30 minutes a day at the start to create a business which could generate you more than what a doctor earns after they work 15 years. This is what I want you to focus on. Give me a month to make your first dollar and a year to make your first $100,000. From there you go forward, and that's working part-time. First, we need to install your entrepreneurial operating system.

The Entrepreneurial Operating System

Perhaps the greatest miracle we've all been exposed to is the thing that's probably within easy reach of you right now: your smartphone. The smartphone is an amazing device. You've got more computing power in that one phone than existed on the planet up to 1985. It's extraordinary. What makes a smartphone and why is this appropriate for an entrepreneur and your own operating system?

For a smartphone to work, for it to do its thing, for it to do all the awesome things that you want it to do, there are three elements that it should have. The first is it must have the right operating system. If you've got an iPhone that's iOS. If you have an Android smartphone that is Android. If you're one of the few people who has a Blackberry or Windows mobile phone, they have their own respective operating systems as well. If you try to run Android on an Apple phone, then you've got all sorts of problems; it's not going to work.

Just having the operating system by itself does nothing. The phone itself does nothing. It needs the OS, it can't function without it, but without apps, the phone does nothing. You need to install the apps to be able to do what you want to do.

Then, of course, just the apps sitting on the phone really mean nothing unless you use the apps. If you can imagine a pyramid, the foundation of the pyramid is the operating system because if you don't have the foundation, you've got nothing. Then there are apps and then at the top, you have to use them.

Guess what. Your entrepreneurial operating system is exactly like that. If you try to install "Android" and you're an iPhone type entrepreneur, then nothing's going to work. This is what's happening with people trying to build a business. There are four different types of entrepreneurial operating system, or eOS. If you're using the wrong one, then it doesn't matter what courses, which are like apps, or how you act, you will not get the right result because your foundation is wrong.

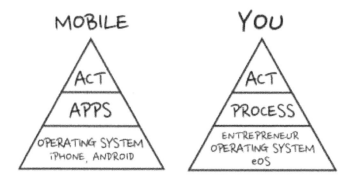

The Kolbe Experiment

It's not the lack of apps, it's not the lack of techniques, it's not the lack of courses that's got you. It's willpower, energy management, and acting to your strengths that's the key. How do we discover our eOS? Well, this is where the Kolbe Index comes into the picture.

Several years ago, I was introduced to the Kolbe Index. I hate personality tests, I really do. I've never taken an IQ test because I'm terrified of the results. The Kolbe Index A test is different because it doesn't talk to you about your emotional circumstances or how smart you are. It just figures out the way you act andwhat your strengths are when you act. It's unique. When I took it, it was perhaps the most comforting test I'd ever taken because it's like Kathy Kolbe, who created the Index, was looking over my shoulder. You know, sometimes you need people to be able to tell you what you should know, but you're too close to it. That's what the Index was like for me.

Now, she doesn't know me from a bar of soap but she was able to define, just by me answering 15 minutes of questions, that I enjoyed speaking off the cuff, that I enjoyed working with video, that I really struggled with writing and I had started many productivity systems in my life and none of them had ever stuck. It was crazy. It was like she was this amazing mind reader!

I discovered I was a "squirrel" entrepreneurial type. I was somebody who's quick to act, didn't like to be hemmed in with processes, and just needed the basic facts to get started. As I was excited about this Kolbe Index, I wondered, "What if we did a test with 200 Challengers? Let's just see if everybody is like me, or are they different?" This was really intriguing, so we did the research.

Of all the hundreds of possibilities, a Kolbe Index number is made up of four digits and they indicate how you act in four areas - fact finder, follow through, quick start, and implementor. You get a four-digit number. Mine is 4-1-9-4, which means I'm a very high quick start and a very low follow through. As Kathy points out, there are no wrong profiles. There are no bad profiles, it's just how you are and it's how you act.

When I think about it, it's how I've always acted since I was a kid. What does this mean? When we did *The Challenge* test, the results were astounding because of the hundreds and hundreds of combinations it turns out there were four, three major ones and one very rare one, that made up our testing base, of Challengers. This was an extraordinary result. What was fascinating was the different types had completely different approaches. If they tried to follow the approach of the other, use their operating system, if you will, of the other type of entrepreneur, it would cause them all sorts of misery. This was the discovery.

What are the entrepreneurial types? Well the first one, which is my one and, by the way, about 65% of you reading this, is called squirrel group. As I've mentioned, this is the type person who is quick and excited to try things, perhaps easily distracted by baubles and objects, which is why I call it squirrel, and always looking for shortcuts. You're looking for ways to buck the system. If you must turn up and do the same thing every single day you become miserable. You've tried a lot of productivity systems in the past and nothing's ever stuck. You love starting them, you get very excited starting them, but nothing sticks.

You're quite happy to try experiments and you're always excited, but maybe you don't track the results. Maybe you don't realize what the value, but if you try to follow a set of processes set out by someone else, you're going to struggle unless you know how to manage your nature and know how to use your operating system.

Thirty percent of you are what we call "research addicts". This is my colorful term for you. Now, you're the opposite to me, but I love you guys and you are just as good entrepreneurs. It's important to emphasize, wherever you fit, you're going to be a great entrepreneur. This is not a judgement; it's just how you act. Once you start acting the way you should, you're going to be way more comfortable and effective!

The research addict is somebody who loves fact finding. They love researching, they love doing the courses, they love studying and really enjoy the process of understanding a market and understanding the needs of a market. They're great, but unfortunately, they also have a relatively low follow through. That means that sticking with processes, they're much better at, but they're far more likely to be comfortable writing. They much prefer to be behind the scenes, behind the camera, than in front of the it. They'd rather not talk off the cuff. They'd rather plan what they should say. Again, completely opposite from me, but there are lots of huge advantages to that too. The research addict makes about 30% of entrepreneurs.

Another 5% is what I call the "process king". These are, in Kolbe terms, high fact finders and high follow-throughs.

These are the people who are actually really good at understanding productivity systems and probably have spent the last little while, if you're still with me, going, "What are you talking about? I'm good at managing my to-do list. I love managing people. I'm really good at that.

"You are good at that, it's awesome. That is fantastic and I envy you immensely.

The challenge for the high fact finders and high follow-throughs is getting you to start something new! You struggle with pushing the go button on a campaign or conducting an experiment or a new funnel or doing a new advertising campaign. When you have to go off script, when you don't know what the result of the process is, it can be a real freeze moment for you. That's okay too because there are ways of working around this.

The fourth type, which is, as I say, super rare, is people who are in the category of "inventors". You have a high implementer score. For everyone else – we are not so good with our hands, not people who would be building and constructing a bunch of stuff. There is a small percentage who are good at this and when I ask they are inevitably inventor types.

Again, fantastic. Of course, with invention and inventor types, they love making the things but then selling and marketing and doing all the testing is the antithesis of what they're all about. Fortunately for you, that's okay; we can work with you as well.

Play to Your Strengths!

Here's the key point of all of this. If you play to your strengths, you'll have more energy, more willpower, and you'll have more fun implementing what you need to implement to build your business. Unfortunately, our entire education system is built around working on our weaknesses and improving them. For years, to give you a personal example, I've tried to write a book. I've tried and tried and tried, and I've never been able to do it. I know it's important, people have asked me to. Publishing companies have offered me money to. I've just never been able to do it.

I realized, with my Kolbe profile, that it's something I just don't have the natural competency. Here's the problem. When I do write, it can be very good. I've had some articles that have been read by millions of people, but it's such a struggle for me to do that. Thanks to understanding my eOS, the way I'm doing this book is by being interviewed, I'm being recorded. This'll be transcribed and edited, and we'll create the book that way.

I've found a process which suits me and my entrepreneurial nature, and this might be something that'll be very exciting to those of you reading this book, as a way of getting around the fact I've never been able to write a book before.

If I hadn't had access to this process, then I wouldn't be doing this. It's playing to my strengths.

Here's the thing: there's never been a better time to outsource your weaknesses. Now I know, because of our research, if you understand the right way to manage people, there's never been a better time to find people who can do the stuff that you're not so good at. For them, it's super easy and it's super cheap for you to be able to do. I know a lot of you reading this have tried outsourcing and failed. There's a good reason for this and we'll address it later in the system.

To give you an example of how this works and how the operating system works, let's look at the productivity system junkie. I'm certainly in this category. I've got a shelf full of productivity systems, day planners, of different types of diaries, different apps, all these sorts of things. I've tried dozens and dozens and dozens and dozens—hundreds probably—of them. I love setting them up, but if it comes to following them, I just never open them again. I have things like Evernote, where I collect things studiously. I put all sorts of web links and everything into Evernote, and I never opened it again.

It's just the style I am. There are other people here who are researchers, but they don't act because they're worried about wasting their time or what will happen if they get the wrong results. Then there's the classic situation of being someone who's comfortable doing video or comfortable writing. Someone who's comfortable with an off the cuff style or someone who needs to plan what they should say.

Now let's tackle this outsourcing problem.

How can you manage when you hate being managed? I promised I'd tell you about this. Here's the thing, most of us who have become entrepreneurs have done so because we hate being managed! Here's the deal: if you hate being managed how can you possibly be a good manager? Right? It doesn't make sense when you think about it. Let me save you a $40,000 MBA right here. Here's what a great manager does. They ask three questions of every person in their team. They ask, "What did you do yesterday? What are you doing today? Is there anything stopping you from delivering what you promised to deliver at the start of the week?" If you ask those three questions, you become a great manager.

Here's the trouble, you should ask that of every single person in your organization every single day. Apart from the 3% of you who are those high follow-throughs who are reading this, we would rather slam an appendage in a car door than do this every single day.

Most of us, because we assume people are like ourselves—that's a completely and natural thing to assume—we think that if we commit, we deliver. If you're reading this and you say, "Ed, I am going to deliver you that design by Friday," you're going to deliver it, by hook or by crook.

Most of us will probably have to set our alarm super early on Friday morning to rush to complete what we promised to deliver, but we will deliver it. We will absolutely deliver it. Here's the thing: we're 5% of the population. 95% of the population doesn't work like this. They're just not wired like that. That's neither good nor bad, it just is.

How many times have you given a task to somebody who's an outsourcer and you said, "Have it done by Friday"? Of course, you leave them to it because you hate to be bothered yourself. You don't want somebody looking over your shoulder every single moment of the day bothering you. You just leave them alone and then when you contact them on Friday to see where the design is they say, "Ah, sorry, I couldn't find the log-in to the iStock photo that I needed to get this design working." "When did this happen?" "Tuesday." They spent three days not being in touch because it's just not natural for them to be able to reach out and contact you.

There is a solution to this because there are people who are wonderful and love nothing more than reaching out to your team every single day. That is a subject for another time.

Right now, if you realize that when you understand how you work (your eOS) and then you take the processes you learn and apply them in the style that works for you using your operating system, everything changes.

The rest of this book will show you how to apply all of that to the creation of your own online business.

Here is the link to take your own Kolbe test: www.yourfirstdollar.com/kolbe

Installing eOS

If productivity systems don't work for most people reading this, how do we possibly get things done? How do we stay organized? This is the incredible challenge. Fortunately, there is an answer. It started way back at the end of World War Two at the car company, Toyota. Now stay with me here because how we get from Toyota, the car company, to you being more productive than you've ever been is a fascinating journey.

After World War Two, Toyota realized they had to make changes in the way cars were produced because quality was so poor.

A car would go right through the manufacturing line and a person who was on the manufacturing line would do one job. They'd do that one job their whole life. Their whole career might be putting a wheel on the car. They never changed their job, so they just did that one thing.

As the car would go through the production line, nothing would be fixed. At the end, when the car rolled off the production line at a Ford factory, all the defects would be fixed at the end of the line. They would have teams of engineers who were highly skilled to be able to fix all the little errors and all the little defects.

Toyota realized this doesn't make sense. Before Toyota the thought of stopping a production line to fix a problem was heresy. If you stopped the production line, you got sacked. The line must move. Raw resources in one end, car out the other end. Toyota said, "No, if we fix the problem, if we actually restrict the number of cars that go through so that we fix the problem when it occurs, we'll actually have much better cars and we will improve our processes over time."

This revolutionized car production and, indeed, manufacturing in general. It changed the world. That's why Toyota became the number one most profitable car manufacturer in the world and their cars consistently have the least number of defects in them. Now, of course, all cars are manufactured this way.

How does this relate to us? Well, we need to look at the industry which has shown the greatest growth in history. If you look at the last few years, there's no question the thing which has shown the most innovation, the most advancement, is software.

We've already talked about the miracle of our smartphone. Cast your mind back 10 years ago, when a program updated and a new version came out, it was a major deal. It might happen every 12 months.

Fast forward to now, how many updates do you get every single day on your phone. The software on your phone is constantly improving all the time. Facebook, for example, updates every two weeks like clockwork. How does this happen? Well, a group of software developers in 2000 had a look at what Toyota had done in their production line in involving the workplace, getting people to love their jobs, switching jobs all the time, making them feel involved with the whole process, and thought, "What if we apply that to software. Would it work?"

Well, the short story is, it worked incredibly. Of course, software is not physical. You can't see what's going on in software, so they had to create a shared visual board so people could see what everybody else was doing on the project, you could see what was going on. That board was called the Kanban board, named after the process that Toyota used to track parts through their system. They literally used physical tickets. Kanban was a revolution. You could tell if parts were getting low because the cart that held them was right next to the worker who needed it

The American car companies spent millions and millions and millions of dollars on software which just had to be changed all the time. Of course, it took years in those days to change the software, whereas a simple ticket that somebody writes on and you could visually look at the line and say, "Wow, that's where all the tickets are. There's a bottleneck right there. We need to figure out how to make that bottleneck not be a bottleneck." It was way more effective and they could make changes overnight. It wouldn't take two years to retool an entire process, so they could afford to stop the line.

Software developers were able to apply this exact same process. The lean manifesto created a revolution in software development. From there Jim Benson and Tonianne DeMarie Barry wrote the book Personal *Kanban*. Jim thought, "Hang on. What if I take all these principles and apply them to individuals? I've never been able to get a productivity system to work. I need to be able to track what's going on, but I've never been able to get it to work. I don't get it. What if Kanban is the answer to that—a visual way of tracking what needs to be done?"

Personal Kanban was born and when I came across the *Personal Kanban* book, it was a revelation. I started applying it to myself. If you've seen any of my videos, you'll notice above my shoulder, in the back of my office where I can see it, is a board with a bunch of Post-it notes on it. That is my Kanban board. If you implement the Kanban board, as now hundreds and hundreds of my students have, and all my private clients have, you will see a dramatic, dramatic change.

What I find is it's often the things that seem the most counterintuitive, that go most against the standard advice, work the best. This first one will blow your mind. We must get you to do less work so you can output more. That's right, less work and you'll achieve more. It's about the concept of flow.

Most of us, when we're tracking things, use a to-do list, whether it be electronic or on paper and pad. We try, it doesn't work that well, but we try.

Think about this for a second. If I were to ask you to find the railway station on a map, I could hand you a map, probably of any city in the world, it wouldn't matter what country, and you could look at that map and you'd see the black line that represented a railway line, or a couple of lines, and you'd be able to see a train station. You'd be able to point to the train station and say, "Yep, look, there's a little symbol of a train. That's a train station." You could probably do it within five, 10 seconds. It may take you 30 seconds to find a subway stop or a train station on a map.

Now, if I gave you a list of every single house and every single railway station and every single business in that city and said, "Please find me the railway station," and you had to go through, alphabetically, and look through this list, which would probably be a sheet of pages, probably 30, 40 pages thick, how long would it take you to find the railway station? It might take you hours, because you must go through until you find something called railway station. That's the difference between seeing something visually, where you can recognize it in an instant, like a map, as compared to a list.

When you look at a to-do list, all you see is this huge amount of stuff that needs to be done. Guess what, at the end of the day with a to-do list, it's still there. The vast majority of things are not done. How do you think that makes you feel? As it turns out, this is traumatic for your brain, but we'll come back to that.

Where have we talked about people being visual and not being so good at following processes – It's highly likely your eOS is attuned to being visual and productivity systems just never stick.

The vast majority of entrepreneurs are very visual in nature. Kathy Kolbe talks about this extensively.

It hit me - what if using a Kanban board like software developers is the answer!

I thought, "Hang on. The big problem with all productivity systems is they are not visual, they're not like a map. They are lists." Often what happens when you tick a list, it disappears or it's just a big list that sits on a notepad somewhere.

It completely doesn't work the way an entrepreneur works. What if we could use this visual process where you could look at a Kanban board, once you know what you're doing, and in a minute, you'll see exactly what you must do next, what's important this week, and how you're doing, how you're going?

Having a visual board was key to the process. It had to be physical because, guess what, entrepreneurs love to be able to get up and pace around. Are you the type of person that loves getting up on a whiteboard and planning things? Or often you'll find yourself drawing and scribbling different things and ideas if you're thinking. Well, you're not alone, that's most entrepreneurs. We're unique in thisway so we need a unique way of visualizing what we must do and a Kanban board does this beautifully.

The second realization, and this is what Toyota figured out, was that at some point in any system, any manufacturing process, there's a bottleneck.

Let's say, for example, it's the engine. Building the engine is the bottleneck for a car manufacturing process. It doesn't matter how many parts you produce, how many bits of inventory you have, if you can build 10 engines a day andyou're delivering parts at a rate of 20 engines worth of parts, guess what, you're going to have a stockpile of inventory and it's going to grow by 10 every single day. That's incredibly inefficient. It costs a lot of money.

Conversely, if you don't get enough parts, everything downstream of the engine building, are sitting around twiddling their thumbs. Customers are waiting for orders because they want the 10 cars and they want the 10 engines to go in those 10 cars. You've got unhappy customers and you've got people who are twiddling their thumbs. It's not efficient.

The most efficient way of working in any manufacturing process, delivering anything, is to work with the bottleneck. You can only work to the pace of the bottleneck. It makes sense to work on the effectiveness of the bottleneck first. Guess were the bottleneck in your business. If you're raising your hand right now you are correct. Spoiler alert: you are the bottleneck.

When you're starting out, you're doing everything. As you build a team, you slowly start to remove yourself as the bottleneck in your business. This is where we want to get to. Right now, as you're reading this, you are going to be the bottleneck in your business, so we have to manage the flow of work into you because you're the bottleneck of the business. Did I mention it YOU are the bottleneck.

Jim and Marianne in Personal Kanban use the imagery of a stream. If a stream is running with the right amount of water, it's a healthy stream. Fish are in it, it's beautiful, the farmers can take water for their crops. Everything works well as a system. Now, if there's too much water, and what's too much water in inventory terms? A flash flood. Suddenly, that's a disaster. The houses along the river get washed out. The fish die because they're just blown out of the creek. The ecosystem of the creek may take years to recover from a flood.

Now, entrepreneurially, we have floods all the time. You're probably in a flood situation, some people call it redlining, right now. You seem like you've got this incredible number of things you have to do all at once—not just in your business but in your personal life, in your health, everything.

The concept of work/life separation is rubbish. It's not realistic, particularly when you're starting out a business. We've got this huge tidal wave of stuff to do and obligations to meet. That's not healthy.

The other way, of course, is what happens if the creek dries up and it becomes stagnant? Then the fish die because there's no water. That's also a problem. Less of a problem in an entrepreneurial business, as a general rule, but it can happen. If we get the flow right, if we understand that your capacity, particularly when you're starting out, if we make sure that you are working to your capacity, or slightly less than your capacity, you will experience flow. That's what we're trying to get.

The Zeigarnik Effect

There's something else that's really super important for an entrepreneur, this absolutely shows why the Kanban board is so powerful. It's called the Zeigarnik Effect.

The Zeigarnik Effect is a process which was discovered by the Czechoslovakian researcher Bluma Zeigarnik. Shediscovered by watching waiters everything we're trying to remember in our heads is using energy in our brains. That's a problem because the more we're trying to juggle—and guess what, as an entrepreneur you're trying to juggle more than most—your ability to actually be creative, your ability to have the willpower and the energy to implement what you need to do is extremely diminished. This is just pure scientific fact.

One of the benefits of the Kanban board is that it gives the entrepreneurial brain permission to relax because it can see, visually, at all times what is on your plate. Now this is why having a physical board is so important. Because, as I hear you say, "Ed, if I put that on a to-do list, doesn't that do the same thing?" Well, yes it does, it actually gives you relief in the moments after you do the to-do list.

Here's the problem, what do entrepreneurs do? They don't look at their to-do list again.

They don't go back to it. They hide it. It just reminds them of all the stuff they haven't done. Guess what, your brain realizes that, so it starts storing them anyway. Even though you've got a to-do list somewhere, it knows you don't use them and this vicious cycle occurs. A Kanban board allows you to be able to do short circuit this process.

Now, here's the thing, there is something else in the Zeigarnik Effect which is a lesser known but far more important thing to know as an entrepreneur. When you complete a task, unless there's some emotional attachment to the task, you'll forget it immediately. Your brain dumps it from your memory because it needs to free up the processing power for the next thing you have to do. If there was no emotional resonance, you are just going to forget it.

Now, of course, what sort of emotional resonance do we have to most tasks during the week that we remember at the end of the week? The bad stuff that happens! We remember when there was a crisis!

I see this all the time working with private students. One week they'll be thinking, "This is the best thing ever! I love being an entrepreneur! This is awesome!" Then the next week, because a whole bunch of bad stuff happened, it'll be the worst, "This is horrible, I'm terrible at this.

I suck. I'm going to go watch *Housewives of Atlanta*." They ride this incredible emotional roller coaster and it's not healthy.

Another example of the Zeigarnik Effect, which a lot of you will appreciate because you are like me with low follow through. I don't know if you ever had to try to fill out an expense report. Now, of course, the organized, the 3% of you reading this, would, as soon as you get a receipt, you'd write on the receipt this is what it was for and every evening you go back to the hotel and you diligently fill out your expense report and it'd be done. It'd be accurate and you'd never have to think about it.

Me, I used to wait until I got on the plane at the end of the trip because I figured I'd have a couple hours to do the expense report. I'd pull out the receipt and I'd be like, "What is this? What is the Oily Duck and why was I there? I have no idea." This is the Zeigarnik Effect in action.

Fortunately for us, the creators of the lean manifesto figured out a solution.

In a traditional to-do list and most digital ones, when we check the task is done, it disappears. On our Kanban board, by having the tickets of the tasks we've done in the done column, at the end of the week, we can actually have an accurate look at what we were able to achieve.

More importantly, we can have a look at a task we didn't enjoy and ask ourselves, "Hey, what can we improve next week?

We can actually have a decent conversation with ourselves about how we're working. I know when I'm working with private clients, it's unbelievable. I can look at somebody's board and see exactly where the bottlenecks are, exactly where the challenges are. That's why youshould be doing a Kanban board. Let's build you one right now.

Step One: The 50-Minute Focus Finder

I got this exercise from my dear friend Dean Jackson. Dean created a brilliant exercise clearing everything that's on your mind and getting you to the point where we can set up your first Kanban board.

Here's how it works. You set a timer for 50 minutes and you just literally do a brain dump of everything you've got on. When I say everything, I mean everything. It's personal, family, health, business, library books you've got to return, whatever it is. The key thing, you have to do it for 50 minutes.

This was very clever. I don't know if Dean had this exactly in mind, but you go through an emotional roller coaster as you go through this 50 minutes and it's always the same. For the first 10, 15 minutes you'll be writing like a crazy person, getting stuff out of your brain. Then you'll go through this lull period where you think you've got everything out and you'll start reading back through the list. You might get a couple little prompts. Then suddenly, about 30 to 35 minutes, maybe 40 minutes, this second wave of stuff hits you and you'll be writing flat out and you won't know where the 50 minutes has gone.

You'll feel so much better after you've got it all down on paper. Why? The Zeigarnik Effect. However, most entrepreneurs will just leave it at the 50-minute focus finder and do nothing else. All that feel good will turn to overwhelm. Well, we're going to change that.

Time to work set your timer for 50 minutes and do the focus finder.

Step Two: Set Up Your Whiteboard Wall

Let's build your board.

To create your wall, we need a whiteboard, a pack of Post-it notes and a Sharpie. It's that simple.

Here's a link to the whiteboard and Post-it notes I use: www.yourfirstdollar.com/tools

You need to place it somewhere where you can't avoid it, where you go to do most of your work. For me it's when I walk into my office, it's right in my eyesight so I always see it. Read this next sentence very carefully. You can't have it in a computer, you can't have it hidden. Don't have it in another room you never go into. It's got to be set up somewhere where you're always going to run into it.

Step Three: Set a Timer for 10 Minutes and Populate the Options Column

Take a whiteboard marker and divide the sections like the below.

Here is a diagram of what your board will look like:

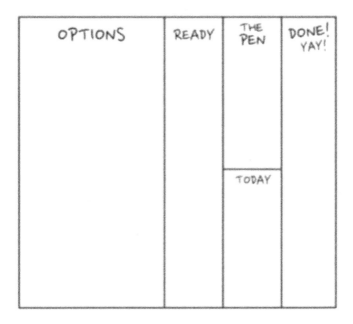

To set it up, there are going to be four columns, and make sure you do them in approximate widths. You've got your options column, your ready column, the pen today, and the done column. We'll explain what all of these do as we go forward.

Now your board is set up, set a timer for 10 minutes and fill up the options column. The options column is the biggest section and we're going to just dump all the important tasks. Again, this is not only your business tasks; this is a personal Kanban. It's for you and you are the sum of all your parts. You've got work commitments, you've got your new business commitments, you've got family commitments, you've got health commitments. Whatever they are, they go here.

Just keep this very broad at this stage, but I want to set the timer. You've just done your focus finder, so you've got plenty of material for this. I want you to write one thing per Post-it note. Now, don't get granular. I know you fact finders will love break down the notes into all the different parts. Don't do this now.

I'm just looking at my board here in front of me and I've got "research creating a Udemy course". Now this, is broken down is a bunch of tasks, but at the moment, in the options column, I've got "Udemy worth a look". That means I'm going to investigate doing a Udemy course.

That's just one big thing. It might be start running or get healthier. Whatever it is, it is. You've only got 10 minutes to fill that options board with all of the things that you are going to be doing, one at a time.

Here's what my options board looks like:

Step Four: Move No More Than Six Tickets into the Ready Column.

Moving something from options to the ready column is the core move of this whole process. Here are the rules. first thing is, whatever the task you have on your ticket (which is a post-it note), it must be able to be completed inside the next week. If it's a big task, using my example of the Udemy course, the very first part is to research the types of courses on Udemy. I would write myself a ticket and put it in the ready column. Something along the lines of "Spend 30 minutes researching productivity courses on Udemy".

I'd place this ticket in the ready column because it's the thing I'm absolutely committing to which I'm going to get done this week. I'm not going to create the whole course, put it up, create the sales materials, and sell it all in a week. I have to chunk down this project. The time to chunk it down is when we move the ticket from our options column to the ready column.

The second rule is you must know what "done" looks like. This is crucial. When you place a ticket into the ready column, you must understand what finished looks like. For example, I've got a ticket here right now which is, "transfer Challenge.co to Hover", which is a domain registrar. I know exactly what done looks like because done will be Challenge. co is at thenew domain registrar. Very, very simple. Whereas if I had a ticket which has "Udemy worth a look", what does this mean? What does done look like? There's no way to tell what done looks like.

Now, if you're researching, I'll give you a great tip. Put a time limit around your research so the ticket is done if you've spent that amount of time researching. Not what you research because when you research, guess what; you don't know what you don't know. It's much better if you're researching to give yourself a 30-minute block. For example, I would say 30 minutes researching productivity courses on Udemy. I would spend the 30 minutes and once I've spent the 30 minutes, guess what; that ticket goes into done.

Now remember the bottleneck. The bottleneck is us, so it's very important that you only put six Post-it notes, six tickets, in the ready column. After we've populated our ready column, we don't look at the options column again at any point during the week. We want to focus on these six key things. Steven Covey referred to it as focusing on the large rocks first. These are the things that we're committing to ourselves to, yes, this is what we want done this come what may. That's the power of the system. Whenever you walk in each day, you'll see here are the six things that I've got to do in my ready column.

Step Five: Move One Ticket

Now move the most important item into the today column and work on the ticket until it's finished. This is key. Because a lot of us suffer from squirrel syndrome and we love switching and swapping. The mental energy this requires is incredibly inefficient. By focusing on this one ticket and asking yourself at the start of the day, look at the context of the day and say, "Well am I traveling or are am I the office? What's realistic for me to work on today?"

Whatever you commit to, do it till gets done. By working on just one thing, you'll blow yourself away with how much you get done over the course of the week

Here's a little tip: I'd block out the hour in my diary I was going to work on my ticket to get it completed.

Step Six: When it's Finished, Move It Into the Done Column.

As you start to pull tickets from today and you start putting them into the done column, it gives you a really great feeling. You've got a visual scoreboard of how much you are getting done. The difference this will make to your productivity, in terms of being able to track what's going on is astounding. They figured this out in Toyota all those years ago, the workers like to see their progress. When you put a scoreboard in front of people, they like to beat their score. We're wired to do it. With your Kanban Board you've got your own scoreboard now in front of you.

Step Seven: Pull the Next Ticket From the Ready Column into Today.

Got some more time today? Great! Pull the next ticket from the ready column and get cracking. Because you figured out the priority at the start of the week you don't waste any energy making a decision about what to do next. Then, if you've finished the six tickets, there's no rule that says you can't say, "Hey, you know what, I'm having a good week this week, let's pull another ticket from the options column, put it into the ready column so we can do it this week."

Here's the thing. Rather than having stuff pushed on you all the time so you're feeling stressed, you're pulling tickets. You are in control. All of a sudden, you're bringing yourself control. The psychological impact of this is absolutely immense. Do this and it will rock your world.

Of course, a Kanban board is not all Unicorns and Hello Kitty!

What happens if you fully commit yourself for the day and then something happens, something you can't avoid? happens with people is they'll fully commit themselves and then something happens and the dam bursts. A dam can hold 100% capacity but as soon as it goes to 110%, it's a disaster because all that overflow water wipes out the village underneath the dam.

Why do they build villages underneath dams? I don't know, but that's what'll happen. It's crazy.

That's what happens to our entrepreneurial lives. It just takes one thing when you are running at 100%. It's also not necessarily a business related thing. Something will happen, you get a call from school and your daughter has fallen off the monkey bars and you have to go to the emergency room. Something happened and then your entire week blows apart. When you're starting your online business, this is when it's most vulnerable. This is where it needs most protection. By limiting the amount of work we do, we end up doing a whole lot more.

If the damn is at 80 % and there is a big storm it won't over fill and the villagers will be saved!! YAY!

If you constrain your work and something crops up you can't avoid, it's cool you can handle it.

This is the power of constraints.
By applying constraints to your Kanban board, you end up doing way more.

I don't know if you watch *Master Chef* or *Top Chef*. They all have these mystery box challenges where they lift the lid off and there's a can of Spam, some cilantro, and eggs. They say, "Right, you have to create a dish in 10 minutes to present to the judges." What's amazing -I've watched thousands of these challenges over the years - I can count on one hand with a couple of fingers cut off the amount of times people haven't, as they say in the shows, '*plated up*', where they haven't put something in front of the judges.

Now of course, it may taste horrible, but never do they not deliver anything. That is just a great example of the power of constraints, which is why I use timers all the time. You'll notice that we've been using timers all throughout these exercises it gives you the constraint which actually promotes creativity. It makes what you do more fun (You high Quick-Start – it's one of the sure fire ways you can execute) and you are more productive with those constraints.

I've created a series of videos for you showing you how to implement Kanban. You can find these at www.yourfirstdollar.com/kanban

Research The Market

It's time to design your business. Let's make it a business worth putting time and effort into, something which excites you. The very first step is to choose a market. You may have something in mind right now—that's great!

Choosing a market can be a real showstopper for getting an online business started. You high factfinder types may not start because you're concerned it won't work or you will waste your time.

Here's the deal.

We are going to give whatever you choose a red hot go for the next 30 days. We will know by then if it's worth moving forward or not. We'll make that decision based on stats and feedback from the market. We are not going to play this game in our heads. If the worst that happens is you fully engage with this process for the next thirty days, it will be thirty days well spent— you'll have learnt the correct way to test a market in the field, learned a bunch of new things, and perhaps most important of all, for perhaps the first time in your life, you've worked in alignment with your eOS. You'll discover what hundreds of clients and students over the past couple of years have discovered.

Applying the correct eOS and using Kanban changes everything. I know of many students who are now using Kanban boards for their family. My eldest daughter uses one to manage her study at school. Regardless of what happens over the next Thirty Days apply these techniques and your life will improve.

The best-case scenario...

You've found a market you want to be involved in, you've researched it, understood the pains, gains, and jobs to be done, created a SAGE download guide (some of you may even do a book like this!!), you've designed and built a funnel to build your tribe, run a traffic experiment and made your first dollar.

So even if the market you choose doesn't pan out, you are not going to be stuck. So pick your market, commit to it and let's roll.

Spoiler Alert: Every Market is a Market

In the old days—way back in 2005—it was important for us to see if your market was online. There were a lot of markets that had yet to come online, and therefore, you had to spend days researching if your market was reachable online. Fast forward to today and yes, every market is a market.

Underwater Kickboxing

When I started teaching the challenge, I had to be careful about mentioning specific niches. If I talked about dog training, within a week, there would be hundreds of dog training sites. It was like the first rule of fight club!

To avoid this, we made up a ridiculous market that could not possibly be true... Underwater Kickboxing. Stupid, right? Go Google it. It's actually a thing, kickboxers use it for training. There is underwater rugby as well if you are interested.

Piano stool restoration, Pottery Valuation and Dog Park reviews—they are all things, they are all markets where someone is making a living. Thanks to the mobile revolution, everyone has access online. When we started the challenge, mobile phones as we know them didn't exist. The iPhone was two years away. (How did we live!?!?)

You can create a business which will make you a living more easily than any time in history—And know you know how your eOS works and is installed. Woof!

Kevin Kelly, founder of *wired* magazine wrote an article which had a profound effect on me and the challenge called "1000 True Fans".

It's pretty simple, if you can find 1,000 people to pay you $100 per year—you have a $100,000-a-year business.

Let's put this into context. Think about your favourite hobby. Have you spent (way) more than $100 on it in the past year? Of course you have. A concert ticket is probably double that these days! This is exciting, we know from research, if you can earn over $70,000, you can pay all your core bills and live well in a western society. Sure, you are not driving Ferraris and living on an exotic boat, but you've wandered into the wrong book if you think that's realistic to do in 12 months.

But 100K a year is super-realistic, and don't forget you're building this while you are transitioning from your existing career. It's part time, not like the 60-hour weeks medical residents do.

Why people struggle with this and why you shouldn't
There is an excellent reason you should pick a market even if you are concerned it won't work.

SCIENCE!

I'm about to save you reading thousands of pages of disruption theory (which is super-cool) to give you this pretty shocking insight.

The Stanford Startup Survey

A survey undertaken by Professor Amar Bhide documented in his book *Origin and Evolution of New Business* surveyed 3500 successful startups and asked this simple question:

"Was the idea you started out with, the idea that made you successful?" 93% of the survey respondents said...

NO!!!

When I first read this, I thought, "Fair suck of the sausage, that's got to be rubbish."

Then I thought back to every successful thing I've ever done.

The Challenge came out of a lark while my biz partner at the time, Frank Kern, was looking after his newborn second child.

I sold my first company for $3.5 million dollars based on a single project we started as part of web development work. Magcast and Scrivcast—the software service responsible for 10 million downloads and 2000 publishers came out of a public company designed to be a business that buys other businesses.

None of these was the reason I started the business they evolved into!!

So, Great News! There is only a 7% chance your first choice of market is going to be right!

"Hang on Ed! Aren't you making the argument we shouldn't rush in and go with our first market choice as we havepretty good odds it's not going to work!!!!"

That's exactly what I'm saying and the reason is SCIENCE!

Well, ECONOMICS!!! To be exact.

Deliberate and Emerging Strategies

Henry Mintzberg and James A. Waters, the prolific economists, explained this phenomenon many years ago. And this is where I've saved you a couple of thousand pages of research. Their revolutionary research which has dramatic consequences for you has the sexy title "Of Strategies, Deliberate and Emergent".

It's ok if you need to take a moment to absorb the full epicness of the title.

Let me break it down in a sentence: "If you don't start something (Your deliberate strategy), the thing which ends up working for you (The emerging strategy) will NEVER appear."

Have a look at this diagram:

If you don't start—and the definition of start is to conduct tests, build your funnel, and interact with your chosen market—the thing which will be your hit will never arrive.

That's why it's called "emerge": It can't if there is nothing for it to emerge from!!

So, a couple of thousand pages of economics has lead me to this conclusion.

You need to pick your market as soon as you finish this chapter. Because if you don't start working, the thing which will make you successful will never appear. That would be sad.

How bad were you the first time?

How bad were you the first time you...? (fill in the blank)

Your answer (apart from being a revealing insight into your personality) gives you the other reason you should pick.

By spending 30 days learning how to start and test your market. You are getting your first legitimate bruises of experience. If it doesn't work out, how much better will you be at your second attempt? Like anything, you need practice.

And know that what follows has been tested in the field thousands of times using the very latest implementation strategies.

Let's start.

What do you love?

This is the obvious place to start. Remember our first law: every market is a market. So we don't need to test if there is a market there.

You are going to be spending a lot of time with this market. Plus, we are designing a business you want to be involved in. So it makes sense to start with what you are passionate about.

Do you have a market you are passionate about?

This could be a really quick section for you. Do you have a market, a hobby, a cause you are super passionate about and want to be involved in?

Great! Job's done. Let's start there. If this was a struggle, don't stress about it, it often is. Let's dig a bit further.

Where do you spend your money?

Remember those thousands of pages of disruption theory I saved you reading? (Hey, I find the study of South Korean hard drive manufacturers page turning awesome!) Well, there is another gem hidden in there. Don't look at what people SAY they want to do. Look at where they spend their two key resources: time and money. We're going to use this fact later on when we look at your market. We're like the Watergate reporters going to "follow the money" in our market. But first...

What are you spending your money on? Some of you will just have enough money to cover the basics (we'll fix that), but it's really interesting. Having spoken with thousands of challengers over the years, it's amazing how people find money for small luxuries. (Starbucks, anyone?)

What are you spending your money on? Set a timer for two minutes and let's do a free writing session.

Simple rule: You are not allowed to stop writing for two minutes. If you are drawing blanks, write I'm drawing blanks. I don't care as long as the pen keeps moving, and yes, I would much prefer you to hand write this exercise because unless you were born after 2007, and good for you reading this if you were!!, you learnt with a pen in hand, your neural pathways at their most creative were formed pen in hand. So use a pen and paper.

If your pen doesn't stop for two minutes, magic happens. You see your brain goes, "WOW! Jane is actually SERIOUS about this! I better come up with something. Usually, I can distract her with Candy Crush or *Housewives of Atlanta* because I know they make her feel good. But okay. Here, this is where you spent your money and huh really—what's all that money on Hamsters and toothpaste?" Or something...

This is another one of those exercises you learn here which will pay off big in all aspects of your life. Thinking in your head is bad. Thinking on paper is productive and awesome; you just need a couple of simple rules. Right. Go do it: two minutes on "Where I spend my money."

Where do you spend your time?

Now that we've figured out where you spend your money, where do you spend your other precious resource: time? We are going to do the same two-minute exercise with the sales rules as last time. The topic: "Where I spend my time."

A couple of tips to make this even easier. I was taught to start with this sentence "I'm going to take a free and easy look at...," in this case, "... where I spend my time." It gets your pen moving and it's designed to take the pressure off the two minutes. It's just writing non-stop for two minutes. You don't have to bring about world peace (although that too would be awesome).

What did you love doing as a kid?

How are you going with your market ideas—any hits? Some people are still struggling at this point and this next one does the trick. What did you enjoy doing as a kid? It might be a while ago, but what you loved doing as a kid when you didn't have all the responsibility you have now is often a good indicator.

Kathy Kolbe makes this clear in her studies: Your index is something you can't work on or improve—it just is. The things you found easier and more fun to do as a kid, you will do now. There is one result I haven't talked about in the

Kolbe Index that did pop up in the study and our implementation program. Some people get a result that is "In transition". This usually occurs when the person taking the test has had a traumatic event in the past couple of years and is looking to get back on track. If this is you, this exercise in particular is important. Remembering your passions as a child could be the key to rediscovering it now after a traumatic event.

You know the drill: Take a free and easy two minutes writing about all the things you enjoyed doing as a kid.

You don't have to be an expert!!

One of the reasons people struggle to pick a market—and it often kicks in around this point, particularly when it comes to our high fact finder friends—is this: "How can I be in this market? I'm not an expert!" Spoiler alert: You don't have to be. What you need to be is an enthusiast. You have to be prepared to respect and understand the market by putting in the research—which we are going to show you how to do shortly.

If you think about it, the best athletes make the worst coaches. The best coaches were poor players at best. They are different skill sets. Now, you should NEVER ever claim to be an expert when you are not. That's bad news and will get you in serious trouble.

One thing everybody has in short supply is time. If you are unearthing amazing content for your market, you'll get all the credit.

Oprah

For many years, the highest paid person on television was Oprah Winfrey. She got there by being enthusiastic about her subjects and being able to make her guest feel comfortable. She wasn't the expert (although she is an exceptionally talented interviewer), her subjects were.

If Oprah recommended a product to her TV audience, it became an instant hit! This is because over years, she built up her skills and she understood the audience. You need to do this too, and in the next section, I'm going to show you how!

In a meeting, who is in the position of influence?

Another way to think about this. In any meeting, on a TV show you watch, who is the person in power in any situation—the person asking the questions or the one answering? Be open to your tribe, invite them on your journey. Just a few minutes ago, I was watching a YouTube channel of a women who decided to take up violin in her 20s and she recorded her progress and created a video showing her progression over a couple of years. She now has a thriving YouTube channel.

She was not an expert, and she still isn't an awesome violin player, but her journey is inspiring (and she is very good, I should add!!). You can do this too in your market. Your ability to relate to your tribe is WAY more important than being an expert.

Smaller is Better

The other mistake which happens here is they choose a huge niche—weight loss, Golf, Dog Training, Underwater Kickboxing. Just checking you are paying attention. For your first attempt, these markets are way too big. It's too hard to figure out the pains, gains, and jobs to be done in such a large market. You use generic responses and general is death!

Big Fish—Small Pond

You want to be a big fish in a small pond. I know this goes against a lot of advice you may have read. I stick by it. Remember, 1000 passionate fans paying you a $100 over the course of a year is a $100,000 dollar business. I'm pretty sure if you're reading this, you don't have a $100,000-a-month ad budget! (If you do, call me!!)

The advantage we have is we can get to know our small segment of a market really well. We understand what makes it tick intimately. We understand the conversations going on in their heads. We understand their problems, their dream results, and the things they need to learn how to do to achieve them.

Let's use a ridiculous example. An example of a big market is weight-loss, a multi-billion dollar industry.

There are also massive organisations marketing in this space. Does that mean we should avoid it? Hell, No! If you are passionate about weight loss and have a strategy that works, go for it. What did Confucius say? "The journey of 1000 miles begins with one step." Well, your path to weight loss domination begins with a single target market.

If you try to tackle everybody with a weight problem, you'll sound generic and will not stand out from the crowd. "Get more energy to do stuff!" "Get your health back!" "Make salad delicious!" (If Salad tasted as good as a Tim Tam, I'd look as buff asfellow Bulldogs supporter and *Thor* actor, Chris Hemsworth!)

Now let's use my ridiculous example of a single target market. Weight loss for Real Estate agents in Phoenix, Arizona. Ridiculous, right? Or is it? "Five take out joints in Scottsdale that have tasty fat reducing fast food you can eat in the car between showings." "How a simple change in diet will get you three extra listings a month." "How your weight problem is affecting your ability to sell real estate in Phoenix and the one three-minute exercise you can do to fix it."

Let's look at another example. Every day, my local florist has at least one salesperson contact them offering to get them "more business!"

Now, most small businesses would like more business, but effectively what my florist is hearing is, "Let me interrupt you from your latest crisis so I can get money from you."

A smart sales person would start with "Hey, do you do weddings?" Weddings are the crack cocaine of the florist business, that 50-buck bunch of posies on Tuesday is worth $150 at a wedding on Saturday! That's the power of paying your small market the respect it deserves by understanding their objectives, their needs.

In both examples, your advantage is knowing the market well. The good news is I'm going to teach you how to do that quickly and effectively.

The Power of Single Target Markets

When I talk to people about this, they get that it makes sense. Unfortunately, the message gets turned in their head and they think that I want them to just focus on this tiny market forever. That's not the case. I don't care if you want to build a 100,000-dollar business or a 10 million-dollar business—you start the same way. Get this one segment right and then move on to the next one.

The greatest business of the last decade is Facebook. They started on one campus (Harvard), and then slowly grew from campus to campus. Then they opened up to select companies, and finally, in 2007 to everyone. Start small and grow from there. Trying to be everything to everybody is death.

Gary Halbert Railway Story

My mentor, Gary Halbert, had another way to illustrate this point. Imagine you are in a railway station at peak hour and you yell out, "Hey You!" No one will turn around. If you yell out, "Hey you in the red jacket," everyone in a red jacket will turn around. If you yell out, "Hey, Ed," all the people named Ed will turn around. We can rig the game significantly in our favour by going small to get big!

Pick Your Market

Alright. It's time to pick your market, there is no wrong choice as the worst case scenario is you will have learned a hell of a lot and ingrained key new techniques that will help every aspect of your life.

Step 1: 10-minute Free Writing Exercise

This is like stretches for your brain (and a 10-minute ticket on your Kanban board is an easy ticket!). You are going to use exactly the same rules as the two-minute exercises we did earlier. Turn off all distractions, use pen and paper, and do not stop writing for anything! Start off with the phrase "I'm going to take a free and easy look at what market I should go into as my first market test."

Like hundreds of thousands of students before you, this exercise will blow you away. There'll be a bunch of jibber, but in amongst, all the coal there will be a diamond. There is always a diamond. That's what's amazing about this process. Oh, and spoiler alert: we run a brainstorming market selection session every couple of weeks you can join in on anywhere in the world! Details to follow.

Step 2: Pick Your Target Market

At this point, you are in one of two states. You'll have your market—your own underwater kickboxing. Awesome! Move along to the next step. If you still can't decide, no stress. There are thousands and thousands who have come before you in exactly the same spot.

So here's what we are going to do. Set a timer for two minutes and write out at least three markets on three pieces of paper. You need at least three. If you only have one idea, that's not a choice. Two ideas are a dilemma, three ideas are a choice.

So you need at least three. Got the three? If the answer is still no, I want you to do another 10-minute freewriting exercise. Set the timer for ten minutes and start off with the phrase, "I'm going to take a free and easy look at why I can't pick a market even though Ed told me it doesn't matter and I've just read a bunch of reasons why it doesn't matter. What is it that I'm really scared of?"

At the end of this ten minutes, do you have an idea? Still no? At the end of this chapter, I'll tell you how to join me on a live brainstorming session from anywhere in the world to help choose your market.

Now remember those at least three ideas for the market to test over the next few weeks, each on a separate piece of paper.

Look at them. Is there one that jumps out at you? Awesome. Lock it in. Still no? I'm now going to give you a technique on decision making that has revolutionised the practice and theory of high achievement and implementation.

Are you ready for this? You will need an open space and it will only take thirty seconds. Crunch each of the ideas into a small ball. Kiss each one and then throw each ball of paper as hard as you can. Go to the one which travelled the furthest and open it. That's your market. "Are you serious Ed?" Deadly.

Here's the science, it's the practice of making a decision that makes things happen. Goethe said it, Tony Robbins said it, but it's not "woo woo" hippy crap. It's the theory of deliberate and emerging strategy as exhibited in the human body. Once you have locked in on a deliberate strategy (the idea ball which traveled the furthest) and you start working on it, taking action, your brain realizes you're serious about it and starts shaping neural pathways to help you access all that stuff you have been absorbing over a lifetime.

Your reticular activations system is activated and all the stuff that can help you which your brain was automatically filtering opens up and you start noticing things that help. So throw the damn idea ball and pick a market. Magic and science will happen.

Step 3: Break Down Your Market

Once you have a market. We are going to do another 10-minute exercise. I want you to think about all the ways you can break down your market.

For example if you chose Golf. Market breakdowns could include:

- Putting
- Driving
- Bunker Play
- Getting out of the rough
- Senior Golfers
- Women Golfers
- Senior Women Golfers
- Breaking 100
- Breaking 90
- Breaking 80
- Golf Travel
- Golf equipment

You get the idea. Each of these could be a market in their own right. The smaller you go, the easier it is to dig into the Pains, Gains, and Jobs To Be Done. The pains of someone who struggles putting are very different to someone who has driving or short game problems.

You can also break down your market by location, occupation, and other demographics (remember the real estate agents in Phoenix who wanted to lose weight!). Think about it. Imagine being a real estate agent in Arizona and I'm looking at two potential books to download, a generic weight loss guide or a guide about real estate agents losing weight in Phoenix. Which would you choose? It's SCIENCE! Not really, but you get my point.

The smaller we start with (and remember this is just the start, as you get bigger, more experienced and more cashed up, you'll start targeting other segments of your market!), the easier it is to be noticed and the more effective you can be. So set the timer for ten minutes and break your chosen market down.

Step 4: Pick a Single Target Market

Now, you need to choose a single target market. In the golf market above, for the next few weeks, I'll focus on putting because that's an area I'm interested in.

So go ahead, set a timer for two minutes and make your decision. Struggling? No Stress! I have a technique.

Write each of the single target markets on a piece of paper (stop me if you've heard this before). Fold each carefully as small as you can without forcing them. Find some sort of receptacle (a hat is considered the most traditional), and withdraw one of the carefully folded pieces of paper. Unfold it. Congratulations, your single target market has been selected and science tells us by making this choice, your chances of creating a successful business have just grown exponentially.

Remember, you're not picking for life, you are picking for a month!! You are learning the process! Change can only happen when you make a choice and ACT on it. Still Stuck? Shoot us an email to ed@yourfirstdollar.com and ask to join one of our free market selection brainstorming sessions—Use the subject "Help me pick a market".

Understand the Market

Remember our super power is knowing our small single target market super well. Fortunately, this is easy.

Now we have our single target market to work with for the next few days, we need to understand our market in very specific ways. Researching and understanding a market is another trap in starting a business. Our high factfinders will never believe they have enough information and may research themselves to a standstill.

My fellow YOLO bros will not do this enough and will barrel into markets without any understanding and find themselves in deep doodoo that could have easily been avoided if they had just taken the time to understand the market. Remember our florist.

The Florist Example

By taking the time to understand that florists' most profitable work is weddings, and it's the thing they want to do more of (A Gain!), we can customise methods and things to help them by helping them get more of the specific type of business they want.

In our putting example, we discover that reading the green and figuring how the ball is going to wriggle around the green is the biggest problem (A Pain!), so we can help with this. An underwater kickboxer needs to work out how to extend their time underwater (remember, this is a thing now!!)—A Job To Be Done.

There are three things you need to understand about your market.

I'm about to save you an enormous amount of time and it's why I'm so confident that, at the end of our time together, you will have the foundation of your business established. Instead of researching yourself to death, there are only three things you need to understand about your single target market. The coolest bit is—by keeping your first market super small—we have saved you an enormous amount of time. In this section, I'm going to show you Pains, Gains, and Jobs To Be Done. You'll discover where to find them and what to look for.

Pains

Someone once said, "You always slow down for the Car Accident. You rarely slow down for the beautiful sunset."

Thanks to a few million years of evolution, we are always motivated to avoid pain.

It makes sense, from running from saber-toothed tigers, to figuring out how to breathe better in underwater kickboxing so you don't, like, die.

Pains don't have to be life or death. A private client I worked with publishes a magazine on Walt Disney World. The happiest place on earth (I know Disney nerds—that's actually Anaheim) surely can't have pain involved. Turns out there are a lot: How to avoid long lines or book the best dinners. You miss out on a bunch of cool experiences because you don't know about them. Arrive at WDW to try your favourite attraction and it's closed for maintenance.

Sure, none of these are life or death, but they are very real issues for someone having a once-in-a-lifetime experience. They want it to be perfect! Typically, our first SAGE piece of content, for your soon-to-be tribe, will be key in helping solve a big point. We are going to use SCIENCE! And build your tribe in the most powerful way.

Gains

Every movie, every book (that holds your interest), course, hobby—anything basically is a story about a journey. You start here, good and bad things happen to you, and you end up somewhere different. You are changed.

Every Story works this way. Bad to worse, bad to worse to tragic to redemption. All of them are some version of this.

A good course, a good video series, an email should have elements of this. In this model, it is where your tribe wants to end up. That changes circumstance, the result is the gain.

When our underwater kickboxer can now train for three minutes underwater instead of two minutes, that's a gain. When our kids score the impossible to get (unless you are in the know) character dinner in Cinderella's castle, these are gains. Every person in your tribe wants to get somewhere. Understanding this is the second crucial piece of information we need.

Jobs to be Done

Bob Moesta and his team created the concept of Jobs to be Done. Their famous example of understanding the job of a thick shake in the morning—convenient for drivers, can be sipped over a commute, filling them up—is fascinating. In our context, we areidentifying the techniques and things people must learn to achieve the gain or get out of the pain we are in.

What are the specific steps for our Underwater Kickboxer to use to increase their lung capacity prior to a workout? What's the secret number you need to call and the exact time you need to call to nab the Cinderella's Castle character dinner?

Now we need to know where we go to find our small target market's Pains, Gains, and Jobs To Be Done.

The smaller the market, the easier this is.

Before we do, I want to emphasize how much easier this next exercise is with a small target market. Remember we talked about the golfer lining up the putt or the real estate agent in Phoenix wanting to lose weight. The key to everything going forward for our next few weeks together is understanding specific Pains, Gains, and Jobs To Be Done. You need different types of fishing lures to catch different types of fish. Don't be scared of tiny. Remember the worst case scenario is this tiny part of the market doesn't work out. You'll have learned valuable techniques and you'll move on to the next part of the market.

Where to find this out

There has never been a better time to find out where the members of your potential tribe hang out. I'm going to give you my favourites here. A word of warning: these groups can be like the Bermuda Triangle of time effort and energy.

In the next section, I'm going to give you very specific strategies for getting the information we need. It can be exciting and full of opportunities for dopamine hits hanging out in these forums.

You are in forums for these four reasons:

- Understand your single target markets pains
- Understand your single target markets gains
- Understand your single target markets jobs to be done
- Look for opportunities to serve

Notice that none of these are "Pimp my stuff"— very crucial!!

Facebook Groups

Facebook groups are my favorite place right now to discover the Pains, Gains, and Jobs To Be Done in a market. You maybe not like Facebook that much. You may not be that interested in Facebook, but let me tell you that's where Joe and Jane Smith are- our target market. They are all on Facebook.

Facebook groups, if you haven't been a part of it, is effectively a replacement for what used to be the old forums. There are groups for literally everything. These groups are a fantastic way for you to be able to figure out those Pains, Gains, and Jobs To Be Done.

The best way to find Facebook groups is using something most people don't even see – the search bar. There's a search bar at the top of Facebook, and if you type in the search bar "your topic group", you'll see a whole bunch of groups, and it very helpfully tells you the numbers in those groups. There are different types of groups as well. There are private and public groups, some groups where you can just join automatically and some groups where you have to apply to join.

At this point in time, I want to do a warning about all the things that I'm about to talk about.

It's absolutely crucial the only reasons you are in this Facebook group or any of the places I'm about to discuss are to learn and to help, not to pimp. You're not there to sell your stuff. You're there very specifically to learn. Make sure you operate this way.

There's nothing worse than seeing somebody who has never been involved in a group, a forum, or a Reddit/sub-Reddit and they start pimping their material without any sort of contribution at all. We don't want to do that. Facebook groups are my absolute favorite place to go. My next favorite place is forums, which, ironically, Facebook groups has tended to replace for Joe and Jane Smith.

The people who were members of forums, which are the traditional bulletin board style groups that have existed for the last 25 years, are your hardcore users in a particular topic. Whereas people who are members of the Facebook group may flit in and out because they just happen to be on Facebook. People who are members of a forum have to physically remember to go to the forum. They have to join the forum. There is a commitment to being in a forum.

These are your more hardcore users, and frankly, they can be your more persnickety members as well. It's even more important to tread carefully when you're involved in forums.

Very simply, to find "forums", go to Google. Type your topic, "forums". You'll be amazed at what you find. Just be careful!

My next one is not a new kid on the block, but it will be new for a lot of you unless you happen to be a millennial reading this. That is Reddit. Reddit is a brilliant forum, depending on the type of market you're involved in. Reddit is again much more the hardcore user in a particular environment. It's far more popular than forums, and it is again probably where people who are on the most cutting edge will be. It's worth doing a search for your topic, Reddit, to find out where it is, and then, it's beyond the scope of this book, but figure out how to use Reddit. I prefer to use Reddit the app on a mobile phone. It's far easier to navigate. It's worth it, if your market does have an active Reddit group, it's probably the single best source of places to figure out Pains, Gains, and Jobs To Be Done.

You can kill two birds with one stone here by looking at Amazon reviews and typing in your market and the word "books" behind it because, let's face it, there are books on pretty much everything, and that's a good sign. It's not something you should be concerned about. In fact, the only time you probably should be concerned is when there are no books on your topic at all.

Here's what you want to do. We want to look at the Amazon reviews. These are gold for figuring out Pains, Gains, and Jobs To Be Done because the positive reviews will tell you all the things that people want to gain. The negative reviews will tell you all the pain points that people have, and you'll also see statements like, "I wish you'd shown me how to do this," or, "I wish you'd go into more detail about that." It's manna from heaven. Amazon reviews is a great place to figure out Pains, Gains, and Jobs To Be Done.

The final one: YouTube comments, but be careful. It's pretty much a cesspit. Having said that, the narrower your market, the more likely it is that you actually have real enthusiasts watching the videos, and the comments will actually a great place to figure out Pains, Gains, and Jobs To Be Done, particularly comments which have received a lot of thumbs up because you can like individual comments. That's really, really helpful as well.

Ultimately, the absolute best way to figure out Pains, Gains, and Jobs To Be Done is to actually speak to somebody in your target audience, to buy them a coffee and have a chat. Go to a trade show where all these people are congregating.

There are trade shows on all the different topics that you could possibly imagine—including kickboxing, I might add. A trade show or actually having the opportunity to speak to people is a fantastic research. The reason I put it last is it's not necessary at this point, but ultimately, it will be the best thing because we want to get customers. Ultimately, we need to sell something, so really understanding your market and speaking with people is a fantastic way to understand Pains, Gains, and Jobs To Be Done.

What to look for.

In this section, I want to give you the type of trigger statements you are looking for when you're going through any of the previously described groups.

If you know what to look for, you're going to save time. Remember, at the start of this entire section, we warned you about researching yourself to death, you research, research, and research, and never actually get involved in the market. By telling you exactly what to look for with Pains, Gains, and Jobs To Be Done, you can set yourself a task over the course of this week just to determine Pains, Gains, and Jobs To Be Done.
Looking for these sorts of statements will help you narrow your search down so you can do this relatively quickly.

Pains: The types of phrases you are looking for things which are painful to your single target market are phrases like, "I hate this. I don't like ... This sucks." You want to look for complaints and frustrations, things which annoy people. The great thing about humans is they're very happy to tell you what cheeses them off.

This is gold for you because, remember, when you are looking at creating a SAGE-style giveaway to collect emails for your tribe, the pain point is going to be our best opportunity to collect an email and help people in our market.

Gains: Gains are where people want to end up. This is where they want to finish their journey or attain a particular goal. You're looking for phrases like, "I wish I could." "Oh, I'm so jealous." "I always dreamed ..." You want to look for things in your market. Where do they want to get to? Another great question to ask is what is their dream result? For the single-target market that you've chosen, what is the dream result?

For our real estate agent in Phoenix, Arizona who wants to lose weight, which was our ridiculous example in an earlier chapter, their dream result is to lose weight, have more energy, be able to get more buyers and sellers. For our underwater kickboxers, their dream result is to win the Underwater Kickboxing Championship or to be able to win more bouts. If they learn to breathe underwater better, they'll get their dream result. Very important information.

Jobs to be Done: These are areas where people want to learn. They want to see how-to's. They want to see checklists. They want to see step-by-step guides. Look for phrases like, "How do I ..." "Do you know how to ...?" "Tutorial requests," and, "Could you please show me how to do this?" All of these jobs are jobs to be done, and they are going to be fantastic for you to utilize as you start to build content in your market. It's going to be useful for products. It's going to be useful for educating people as you take them down the path of becoming a client.

Action Steps

Step One: Spend 30 minutes discovering the best sources for your single-target market.

Here we're going to write ourselves a ticket for our Kanban board. We're going to set a clock for 30 minutes, and using the methodology I described above. We're going to do a Facebook search, a Google forum search, and Amazon Books. You have 30 minutes to find where your single target market is hanging out online. It's a race. You've got 30 minutes. One 30-minute session will get that done for you.

Step Two: Get some 3x5 cards.

Get some 3x5 index cards and create a Pains, Gains, and Jobs To Be Done index card box. Why not digitized? As we discussed already, for the vast majority of you, if you use something like Evernote or some sort of digital collection service, you'll never go back and look at anything that you've collected in that service again.

It's important to have something that's visual. As my mentor, Gary Halbert, used to tell me, he loved to fondle his index cards. It's very important. You physically write the information down, which helps you with your memory and retention. By dividing your index card box into Pains, Gains, and Jobs To Be Done, you're making a collection and will be able to use these cards in a very visual way, which, as we know for the vast majority of you reading this book, is going to be very important.

You need to get those. Here's an Amazon link to my Amazon Wishlist which will enable you to get the cards and card box that I use and recommend: www.yourfirstdollar.com/tools

Step Three: Create three tickets for this week's Kanban board on Pains, Gains, and Jobs To Be Done.

You're going to spend 30 minutes researching each. This is very straightforward. I want you to spend a total of 30 minutes researching the places where you have found, and I want you to do three passes: one pass for pains, one pass for gains, and one pass the jobs to be done.

You have 30 minutes for each pass. That's right, a total of one hour and a half, 90 minutes to figure out the initial run of pains, gains, jobs to be done. Remember, here is a huge trap people have ventured down the path of researching their market, and they've never, ever returned. I'm looking at you, high fact finders. You need constraint, and you need to make this a game for you to do it.

Just like a great *Master Chef* Mystery Box Challenge, you've got 30 minutes for Pains, Gains, and Jobs To Be Done.

We also know, thanks to the great research of Malcolm Gladwell in his book *Blink*, that your first impressions about what Pains, Gains, and Jobs To Be Done are usually right.

There's no need to research ourselves to death.

Step Four: When you do your research, go for quantity, not quality.

You read that right. I want you to set yourself a target for at least 10 3x5 index cards, one pain point, one gain point, one job to be done point for each. For each 30-minute session, I want to see a minimum of 10 cards. The more, the better. If you get 30 cards in each, I'll be so proud of you. That will be awesome. Why? Why do we want to go for quantity and not quality?

I want to refer you to this great example from the book, *Art and Fear*, of an experiment that was conducted in San Francisco pottery class. The class was divided up into two groups, and the pottery teacher gave the first group a standard assignment. "You have a week. I want you to produce one fantastic pottery piece, and that is what you will receive your grade on."

To the second half of the class, the pottery teacher said, "Your grade will be determined by weight. If you deliver 40 pounds of pottery, you get an A; 30 pounds, you'll get a B; 20 pounds, a C, and so on." One side had to do their best work, and the other side just had to go for quantity. They had to create 40 pounds, and that's a lot of pottery, to get the best grade they could.

At the end of this process, they then had outside pottery valuation experts come in and grade, from their perspective, the best pieces. Can you guess where the top 10 best pieces came from? If you guessed the quantity section, you are absolutely correct. People who were obsessing over their one piece didn't even get close, but the people who were going for quantity, inside all that coal, there was that diamond that made everything worthwhile.

When you're doing these exercises, when you're looking at Pains, Gains, and Jobs To Be Done, I don't want you to think about, "Oh, it's just really good pain," or, "It's just an average pain." "Oh, I don't know. I think this might be ... Really, ah, I just don't know." I don't want you to edit at all. I just want you to go full quantity. The more cards you have the better. Go for quantity.

Step Five: Create a New Ticket to rank.

Spend 10 minutes ranking your Pains, Gains, and Jobs To Be Done from biggest issue to littlest issue. We will take 10 minutes for each groupso there are three 10-minute sections in all: 10 minutes for pain, 10 minutes for gain, 10 minutes for jobs to be done.

We're going to take out our cards from our index box, in this case, pains. I want you to lay them out on the table, floor, or wherever is handy, and I want you to set a timer for 10 minutes, and then I want you to sort just based on your gut instinct what you think the biggest pain is. Then you rank it down to what the least painful or perhaps annoying thing is in that market.

I just mentioned Malcolm Gladwell's book, *Blink*. The science regarding this is we know the vast majority of times, you're ranking is going to be pretty good so let's not stress. Spend 10 minutes. I know you high fact finders are probably having a big of a fit right about now, but this is the way you get success, because I want you to focus on the process. It's not the outcome which is important here. The process of doing this is what gets you the tic. It's what gets you the gold star.

Step Six: Put them back in your research card box in order.

Now that you've got them ranked, put them back in your box in order, and you'll see we'll be using that box for a whole bunch of stuff as we go forward.

This seems like an awesome time to mention I do a podcast focused on helping people through the Your First Dollar process! You can find out all about it here: www.yourfirstdollar.com/podcast.

You can even become a guest on the podcast where I can help you with any of the Your First Dollar process

Building a Tribe

When I say "building a tribe," I really mean building a list so you can serve your market. Right now, today, an email list is the most valuable asset you can possibly have. I do believe that, in the future, instant messaging and texting will take over from email. That's not today. Today, when we look at building our tribe, my friend Ash Murya, talks about creating a happy customer factory.

In a happy customer factory, your raw materials are an email address. If we don't have an email address, we have no way of having a discussion with our clients. An email is absolutely the most vital thing. How do we do this? We need to help people with the biggest challenge they have in their market. In return for this help, they're going to be thrilled to give us their email and, more importantly, look forward to getting a further email from us. That's really exciting. Of course, there's a process to it.

This is the first time we are needing to do some technology, but don't stress. We use a super easy service which handles everything for you and is free to start, so you can make sure it's working before you have to pay. We can also get somebody to help do the tech for you so you can focus on helping your market first. In fact, let's focus there, and we'll get to the tech later.

Step One: Let's Start With the Biggest Pain.

Pull the first card out of the pain section of your index box. This was the biggest pain you discovered in your research and it's what we're going to use to help build our email list. Why do we use the biggest pain first?

"Everybody slows down for a car accident, and very few people slow down for the beautiful sunset." It's human nature to focus on getting out of pain first, this is one of the easiest ways we can get attention. Also, you have positive feelings toward people who have helped you get out of pain or showing out how to make the pain better.

That'sall we need to do. I know already some of you are thinking, "But Ed, I just barely know this market at all. I'm no expert. I've been doing this research for approximately two hours."

Stay with me – I have your back.

Step Two: How Can We help With This Problem?

The most important thing you have to understand is you don't have to be an expert. You do have to be an enthusiast; you do have to be someone who's excited about learning.

I often tell the story of the chiropractor. If you've been suffering chronic back pain for the last decade, and you notice there's a new chiropractor who has moved into town, and you say, "You know what, let's give the new her a go, and hopefully she'll be fantastic." You go to the new chiropractor, and it's a miracle. She is brilliant. "Oh, my goodness! For the first time in a decade, I have no pain. This is amazing."

Of course, what would happen when you do that? You tell everybody about it, right? When you're talking to your good friend about it, they say, "Oh, yes. I know her. You must have been her first client. She'd just graduated from chiropractic school." Here's the thing: If you'd known you were going to be this person's first ever professional client when they're out on their own, and you've had chronic back pain for 10 years, would you have you gone to them? No, of course not. You wouldn't have.

They solved your problem, so you don't care about their background. You don't care about how many years (or no years) they've been practicing. They helped you with your problem. You're thrilled. You're thankful, and that's what we want to take advantage of here.

Often when we're talking about solving pains in this context, we're not solving them completely, although that's awesome if you can.

We want to at least pointing people in the right direction. Do you know how to help? This is our first part of this. If you know how to help, this is great, and we can create a small, simple checklist or guide to create, to give away for the email.

What if you don't know? You have to research, and we're going to talk about that very shortly. If you know how to help, you want to create a SAGE checklist. SAGE stands for Short, Actionable, Goal-oriented, and Easy. Think about it. People don't have time to watch hours of video, even though they could be really, really useful.

If you offer some sort of free consultation to people, they think that's some sort of code for a sales conversation, which it typically is. A webinar, they have to be able to go and spend time. Before they even get any sort of help or feedback, it's going to take them a whole bunch of time. Or you can have some sort of very simple, small checklist, a two-page guide that people can download and use immediately.

There is an advanced version here. The best thing, and in fact you're experiencing it right now as we speak, what's working the absolute best right now is to create a book and have a book as a giveaway. It actually meets all the criteria. I know what you're thinking, creating a book is super hard, and that's what I thought for two decades as well, but using this amazing process, at www.90MinuteBooks.com, I have actually created the book you are now reading, which is helping you!

If you've got some resources, it's is a fantastic way of helping the market. If we're starting from scratch, a short checklist is going to be fantastic. Is there a magic trick? Do you know something which can help people really simply and quickly? Again, I'm talking to people in the market who already know what they're doing. Don't worry. If you don't know, I'm going to help you very shortly.

The example I like to use here is a photography. There are a couple of things I can show people, and they're instantly taking better photos. The first thing is to teach people the rule of thirds. If you image three columns and three rows on your viewfinder, so whenever you're taking a photo, imagine a window pane that has three columns and three rows. If you place the subjects of your photo where those panes, intersect, which you'll notice is not in the middle of the frame, you'll instantly start taking better photos. You'll notice this.

Now I'm going to ruin watching TV forever for you. In news broadcasts, any scene, you'll notice that the people who are talking in a scene are on these lines. They're not dead center in the camera. The dead center actually looks really weird, yet most of us try to get the subject right in the center of the photo. By knowing that, it has just taken 30 seconds or so to read this, you'll take much better photos.

The second rule is a great one, "Fill the Frame". Whatever the subject is you are a taking a photo of, just move closer to it or further away so it fills the frame and you don't have any rubbish or anything outside of the subject of your photo. Start doing this, you'll instantly take better photos. This is something you can test literally in 30 seconds with your camera phone right now, and you'll take better photos. That's what I mean by a "magic trick": something you can show people andthey go, "Wow! That is really, really cool."

You may have that. It might be for our underwater kickboxers, it might be a particular breathing technique which increases your ability to hold your breath by 50% just by using this particular phrase.

Whatever it is, it should be cool.

You may, for example, know some YouTube videos which are really good, not done by you, but by somebody else who really helped you understand this particular pain when you were first starting out.

What if you don't have a clue? You've got no idea about what this thing should be. You've got no idea how to solve this pain point on your index card. Great news: We're going to fix this right now. The first thing you're going to do is create a ticket. Spend 30 minutes finding the answer to this pain point. You're then going to create another ticket for your Kanban board. Forum post: What's the best way you have solved this problem?

Yes, this is really cool. I know. The first thing you're going to do is search your Facebook groups and search your forums. They all have search functions to see if somebody indeed has answered this question, and most importantly, has had responses from people saying, "Ah, this is great. This is fantastic. That's excellent." If you find this first up, beauty. Job done. That is awesome, right? You know already, and you've taken 30 minutes of searching on a forum or in your Facebook group to figure out the answer.

If for some reason you can't find it, then ask a question on the forum and say, "Hey, guys, I'm trying to figure out how to solve this," and explain the pain, and see what responses you get from people. Let the forum tell you. That is a huge checklist and wonderful value creator. People love to help out, and asking people who are dealing with the thing every day is a great way to figure out what is possible.

114

Just don't jump to this second step first – spend a good thirty minutes researching first. Nothing will get you a negative response than not respecting the forum and asking a question which has been answered.

Step Three: Create the Giveaway.
They may point you to resources. They may point you to YouTube videos. Great. Just create a nice, one-page document, which is a link to the best articles, the best YouTube videos, maybe the best podcast for solving this particular problem. You've just saved your new tribe member an enormous amount of time.

I would always make the download look pretty by providing the links to a graphic designer on Fiverr and pay them $5 or $10 if you're in a rush, to make the checklist look really nice so you've got a really nice checklist people can use. Boom! It's done. You've created your first SAGE download we can use for testing.

If you need help with this, send an email to ed@yourfirstdollar.com, subject "I need help with my funnel!"

Step Four: Create the Funnel.

First of all, let's describe what a funnel is. If you think about a funnel where you're trying to pour water in a container, you use the funnel so you can capture all of the water and have it, in a controlled way, go into your container so you're not spilling stuff everywhere. We want to do the same with people who are interested in our topic. We want to ask people in our single target market who may be interested and who we can help and we would like to serve by getting their email address. That's what a funnel does.

There are a number of components to this. The first component is the opt-in page. I know you've seen this because the reason you're reading this book is you submitted your email to an opt-in page. This is where the opt-in page is very simple. For mine it was the picture of the book and what you would get out of the book and a download—very, very simple. It's a way of somebody giving you their email address, and in return, you give them your, in my case, book or perhaps in your case, your SAGE giveaway you've created.

The second thing you need is some sort of auto-responder. An auto responder service is the service which collects the email, collects your database of customers, and enables you to automatically send emails.

For example, sending people the information where they can download their giveaway you've just promised them

In an ideal world, all of these things can be found in one place and for free. Fortunately for you, exactly the same service I use when starting a new niche from scratch is available to you to. www.GoGoClients.com does all of these things and it does it very simply. The best part is it's free for a month to try. Before you want to commit to a particular market, you can everything for a month, which is more than enough time to test a market.

Because things change from time to time, I've created a series of videos to show you exactly what you need to do, step by step. You can get these videos here at www.yourfirstdollar.com/funneltools

Do you want my team to do this for you? Just shoot me an email ed@yourfirstdollar.com with the subject, "I need help with my funnel."

Step Five: Your First Test!

Get excited! Don't be scared. Remember, the trick is to complete the process. The results of this don't matter. For those of you high fact finders out there, please don't stress. Following the process is the victory.

Here's what we're going to do. We're going to spend $20 on Facebook to test our small funnel. We're going to target a very small group very, very safely.

What do we need to create? We need to create an ad. Guess what? The copy for the ad has pretty much been written for you because you've got your first pain point, your index card, and your opt-in page. If, for example, our market was underwater kickboxing, and we wanted to help people breathe 50% longer Our ad simply says, "Discover a way to increase the time you can hold your breath by 50%. Click here." Very simple.

You need to have an image that you can use as well. Because things change all the time with Facebook, I've created a series of videos you can watch at www.yourfirstdollar.com/traffic to see the latest methods to advertise safely. You can follow these videos to create your ad and we will send the traffic to our opt-in funnel at GoGoClients. We'll set a small budget (around 10 dollars) and see what happens!!

One of the reasons I love testing with Facebook is that you can test with such small dollar amounts.

Believe it or not, even the biggest advertisers in the business start out testing Facebook this way. It's actually a really big trick. Some people go and throw a bunch of money at Facebook initially, and it actually hurts your results. You want to start really, really small.

Once we have our opt-in page for our download, we've used GoGoClients to create it, then they're going to turn it on. Within a short period of time, within the next 48 hours, you're going to get your first email, and it's time to celebrate. You've got your first tribe member. If you want my team to do this for you, just shoot me an email to ed@yourfirstdollar.com with the subject "I need help with my funnel."

Step Six: Review and Adjust.

We need to look at our numbers. It's very important. Now I'm talking to you high quick starts who'd just like to see if there's an email address and forget about all the detail. We want to look at how our ad is working. Our key metric here from a Facebook point of view is click-through rate or CTR. You want to make sure your ad is producing at least a 1% click-through rate. That means of every 100 people who see your ad, either on their mobile phone or on their desktop, at least one clicks the specific ad. That's our click-through rate.

If you're getting more than 1%, this is great. If you're getting less than 1%, we need to change the ad for our next experiment. We need to try a new headline because we're not getting enough attention. If you're getting above 3%, that's incredible. That's awesome. We're only looking for above 1 in a 100 people who see the a.

Our next step is to figure out how our opt-in page is working. The great thing is GoGoClients provides all this information for you. We want to look at the conversion rate, in other words, how many people arrive at our opt-in page, but then leave us an email? In here, we're looking for above 30%. Above 50% is awesome, and for book opt-ins, we are often seeing anywhere from 60% to 70% opt-in rate.

If we are not getting at least a 30% opt-in ratewe need to tweak the page. We need to change the headline. Why 30%? Of every 10 people who come to our page, we'd like to see three people sign up. Think about it: If they've been surfing on Facebook and they've actually interrupted their Facebook surfing, because they've been intrigued by your ad.

"Yes, I want to learn how to breathe 50% extra," then they don't get your guide, it seems crazy because they've actually interrupted themselves.

That's why we want to see a decent opt-in rate. Guess what we're going to do? We're going to create a new experiment based on tweaking our headline. Depending on our click-through rate and our conversion rate, we can then create a new experiment to see if we can beat our conversion. We rinse and repeated this process.

Offering Products and Services

How do you go to educate your market? You need to pick a weekly way to communicate with them. This is when Dean Jackson came up with an amazing solution. He has an email marketing solution you definitely need to check out at: www.yourfirstdollar.com/emailmastery

When I learned this from Dean, it rocked my world. Here's the thing: Of any given market of 100% of people who give you their email, 50% of them won't buy from anyone ever. Again, check out the link above for the more detail on this. I don't want to take too much time here, but I do want to tell you the key results of this.

Fifty percent of people won't buy at all. Of the 50% left, 85% of those people will buy something in your niche at some point in time over the next 18 months. The other 15% who are left want to buy something pretty soon in the next 60 days.

The vast majority of people aren't going to buy from you right away. We need to create something whichis going to help educate them and enthuse them to want to raise their hand to let you know they are ready to take the next step. You need to pick a weekly way to do this. Once a week, there needs to be some sort of communication.

Your Kolbe profile, which we talked about in the very first section, will help you. If you are like me, there's a high quick start, low follow-through. Video or podcasting is going to be way more useful for you. If you're a high fact finder, maybe an email newsletter or something written is going to bebetter.

Here is what I do. Please remember to keep your own Kolbe in mind because you need to do this consistently. It needs to be done on a weekly basis. Consistency is vital for this part of the process, so you've got to enjoy doing whatever you decide to do on a weekly basis. It's not about doing massive volumes, by the way. It's about being helpful every single week.

My absolute favorite is a podcast, and this is what I do. You can use a podcast to be able to answer questions, to talk to people in your niche, to create interviews. It's a wonderful, wonderful thing. For those of you who are podcast fans, you already know what it is.

When I think about the pieces of content I most enjoy receiving every single week, it's without doubt podcasts. I spend more time within the podcast than anything else because I'm walking the dogs every day and I listen to the podcast when I walk the dogs. When I'm driving or I'm waiting, I'm waiting with my daughters, I'm listening to the podcast.

Creating a podcast which is outside the scope of this book. I'll provide a link at the end of this section to give you my favorite resources for all of these things for learning how to do each one. A simple newsletter may be the best thing for you to do to start. The great thing is with www.GoGoClients.com, you've got all of this functionality built in. You could send out an email on a weekly basis, helping people, pointing them to quality content or maybe short articles.

You could also, like all the kids are doing these days, create a YouTube channel. YouTube has been phenomenal, and when you think about the amount of time you spent watching YouTube. More importantly, think about all the millennials in your life, how much they're watching YouTube. I'll tell you right now, my kids are watching way more YouTube than they watch television. This is the future. If you're so inclined, a YouTube channel where you publish videos on a weekly basis could absolutely be a fantastic way to keep the 85% educated and entertained.

People feel really comfortable doing this free stuff because they don't have to do anything scary like asking for money. This is a bad mistake mistake, and this next section will help you avoid the number one mistake people make when making free content.

You can learn about my Podcast designed to help you every week here at www.yourfirstdollar.com/podcast
Along with some of my favourite resources, I also talk about the podcasting gear I use at www.yourfirstdollar.com/tools

Don't give free hugs

I want you to imagine something. I want you to imagine that you're going to your parents' if they're still around. I know my mother-in-law makes these amazing dinners, so for the last 15 years, I've been going to my mother-in-law's place for Easter and for Christmas. My goodness, the spreads are just... I'm getting excited just thinking about it right now.

It is amazing, and I love it. She makes my favorite chocolate ripple cake dessert. It's awesome. Just imagine that the next time I go there for Christmas Day, I say, "Marlene, this has been fantastic. Thank you so much for another amazing effort." She says to me: "Ed, that's awesome. I'm so glad you loved that. That will be $35." What? "What just happened here?" When I tell this story in workshops, people physically recoil and laugh and think, "Ha, ha, don't be silly."

What people who create a YouTube channel, blog or podcast do is create all this free content—free hugs, as we call them—and then, all of a sudden they start charging for something their audience has been getting for free.

You say, "Hang on, Ed. I spent 12 months researching this new course. I've interviewed experts. I spend thousands of dollars of travel. I put it together, why shouldn't I charge?"

The problem is, your market doesn't know or frankly care about all of that. At the end of the day, they see text, digital text, videos, PDF, stuff that you've been giving away for free, and now all of a sudden you're charging. That's why the market goes Bananarama when you do this.

The great Dean Jackson solved this so elegantly. He has a methodology called, "Do you want a cookie with that?" Again, I'm not going to explain it in detail here. You can hear it much better from the great man himself www.yourfirstdollar.com/emailmastery

Somewhere in your free content, you need to ask people to raise their hand to let you know that they're prepared to take the next step.

For example, using our underwater kickboxer, we have a course now we've created which is a guide to increasing your ability to hold underwater breath by 50%.

Let's call it a workshop where people come into our special underwater kickboxing training facility in Thailand, and they train with us for a week. At the end of each podcast we do on our underwater kickboxing, I'll say something like, "Hey, are you ready to increase your lung capacity – get this 7-step guide to increase your breath hold time by 50%"

By simply asking, as Dean would call it, "Would you like a cookie?" you're letting people know, yes, they're getting amazing, valuable content, but there are also paid options to increase and enhance their experience or help them implement what you're teaching.

That's the key one simple little change with your weekly communications which makes all the difference, and you don't have the, jarring response when you offer a product to your list if you're used to getting free stuff all the time simply by asking, "Would you like a cookie?"

A great way to come up with cookies is think about what would be the next step for your particular market. This is the key question you want to be asking for the cookie. Where do we get topics for what we're going to put in this content? Guess what? You've got an index card box full of them.

Remember when we did all our Pains, Gains, and Jobs To Be Done? All you need to do to come up with topics is to flip through, maybe even randomly, close your eyes and randomly pick a card. That can be your topic for the week. Of course, as you get involved in the market, you want to become a collector of Pains, Gains, and Jobs To Be Done.

I have a little cardholder for my 3x5 cards which I take with me everywhere so I can jot down, and if I hear a pain, or a gain, or a job to be done, I can jot it down and put it in my card box collector for that particular project. I'm constantly collecting things. Then of course you can make a note on the index card where you addressed it in a podcast, a newsletter, or a blog post so I've got something of value to send to people to help them out.

By the way, we hold brainstorming sessions every couple of weeks on ways that we can serve our markets and cookie creation. If you'd like to join us, just send an email to ed@yourfirstdollar.com and we'll let you know when our next brainstorming event is.

Making Your First Dollar

If there's one part of the process which has changed over the years of me doing the challenge, it's how much easier creating a product has become thanks to outsourcing and using services like Fiverr. but before we build a product we need to test whether the market is prepared to buy something.

The big mistake people make is they lock themselves away for eight months writing their epic book, or their amazing course, or their incredible video series. They release it to the world and then have the horrible discovery, nobody wants to buy it in the first place. Instead, we want to take from our agile methodology we talked about with our Kanban board to create what is called a minimum viable product. This is the minimum thing we can create or use to test our market to see if there is desirability for the problem we want to solve.

Will the market buy?

The awesome thing about online businesses is typically we can use affiliate products—in other words, products already serving our market which we like, that we've used ourselves, it could be a book, or it could be a video series.

It could be anything, but it's an affiliate product, so we can see whether our market is actually buying.

If you create surveys and do all those sorts of things, that's one thing, but when you see people spend money, that's when you know you are on a winner. The great thing about testing your market is identifying an affiliate product, and the best way to do this is to Google your single target market affiliate and see if there's anything that comes up.

My other favorite is just to use Amazon and to use a book on the subject that you've really loved because, again, we're not aiming to be rich here. We're just testing to see whether our market will buy. Guess what? This is also the most awesome way and the quickest way to make your first ever dollar in your new online business.

Because this changes all the time, I've created a video at www.yourfirstdollar.com/amazonaffilate to show you how to set up as an affiliate on Amazon and to run our first test using www.GoGoClients.com.

This is an exciting stage because when you make your first book sale, you only need to sell a couple of books and you will have made a dollar!!

Remember before you can make $100,000, before you can make $1 million, you need to make $1.

If you see there's a certain percentage of people who are buying this book, you know there is an appetite in this marketplace.

I don't want you to even think about creating your own product until you've built your list up to 1,000 emails. For sure use affiliate products. For sure promote other people's stuff you think is going to help your tribe and it's going to be useful for people, but when you reach 1,000 emails, that's time to thinking about creating a good product to design for your market.

We don't want to go and create our product right now, because why risk it? In this day and age, there is no need to risk creating a product first before we sell it.

So what can you do to test your own product without building it? There are two amazing strategies that you can use. The first strategy is sales page beta testing. What you can do is create a sales page for your product. Just don't build the product. Send traffic to your sales page and see how many people will register for a waiting list and this is an excellent indicator to demand for the product. If they won't leave an email – they sure won't buy!

If you want help on product development and product planning, we have a brainstorming session we run every month on creating products, and product development, and talking about sales page beta testing. I you want to join us – just send me an email ed@yourfirstdollar.com, and we'll let you know when our next session is.

Sales page beta testing is where we design what we think our product will be. We'll create all the features and the benefits. We might create a sales video. We talk through it all. We have a "buy" button on there, and you can do all of this through GoGoClients, but instead of taking people's money, we say, "Look, thank you." When they go to the buy page we say, "Thanks for your interest. The product is in beta at the moment, and we'll let you know when it's available."

That is going to give you some fantastic data about how good your sales pages are, how much interest there is in the product. That's one way that you can test a product without actually having to build the product. This has become incredibly popular, and instead of spending potentially months on a new product, you spend a week creating a sales page for the product.

The second idea, and this is a huge trend, is crowdfunding. Once we're up to 1,000 emails, we can potentially take pretty much the same sales page we create for testing and use it for crowdfunding. Once we've figured out there is interest for this, we can then turn it into a crowdfunding campaign. Or you can go straight to the crowdfunding campaign. It's up to you.

A crowdfunding campaign is very similar to a sales page, but the great thing about itis you say, "Okay, here's the product. I'm going to create this new underwater kickboxing breathing guide, and I'm also going to create this new underwater breathing apparatus, a new type of snorkel that is going to be used for underwater kickboxing."

I figure it out. I do all my planning. I figure out what it's going to cost, what the time frame is. I plan the whole product out, source it, do prototypes, all those sorts of things. Before I build it or commit to any of it, I create a crowdfunding page, and here's what happens. I set a card for this to be worth my while, I need to raise $10,000. What I do is create a crowdfunding campaign, and one of two things happens. I let my audience know about the crowdfunding campaign. In fact, I let them know well before I even start the crowdfunding campaign that I'm thinking about doing a crowdfunding campaign and, as I said, one of two things will happen.

One, if I hit my $10,000 goal, I have the money to build my product, and now I go about building it, and by the way, people are trained with crowdfunding not to expect the products straight away. They are trained to wait for the product, so you've been paid for the product. Now you go about creating it. For those high quick start/low follow through amongst us, this is the perfect way to ensure you get your product done because you've got people who've paid you money to make sure it's delivered. Itis a brilliant motivator for you.

Or if it doesn't get funded, guess what? You didn't hit your market nail on the head. No stress. Everybody gets the money they committed back and you can modify things and go again. Many of the most successful Kickstarter projects of all time didn't work on their first go, but you don't have to risk all the time and effort of product creation before you know it's a success.

As I mentioned, we have an amazing monthly brainstorming session where we talk about product and brainstorm product development ideas and all the things to do with creating products. If you'd like to join us on that, please send an email to ed@yourfirstdollar.com, and we will figure out the best way forward for you.

Here's How to Make Your First Dollar in 30 Days and Your First $100,000 Inside of 12 Months...

You already know you want to start an online business. You may have already tried, but something never clicks. Juggling a day job while you build your dream life can just be too difficult.

That's where we come in. We help you crack the code by installing an 'operating system for the entrepreneur' to get you the freedom of a successful online business.

> **Step 1**: We help you understand what type of entrepreneur you are, so creating your business becomes effortless.

> **Step 2**: We help you figure out which market you'd love to work in and help unlock the formula to having people want to work with you.

> **Step 3**: We show how to quickly to build your list and gather your tribe before guiding you to build an offer, product and services your tribe will love.

Most entrepreneurs quit their online business right before they're successful because they don't recognize their flawed operating system.

Now it's time to get cracking – Download your EntrepreneurOS checklist to guide you step by step through the first dollar process:

www.yourfirstdollar.com/checklist

Make sure you let me know when you make your first dollar – ed@yourfirstdollar.com. I can't wait to read you story.

25633538R00085

Made in the USA
Columbia, SC
01 September 2018